Urban Planning

URBAN STUDIES INFORMATION GUIDE SERIES

Series Editor: Thomas P. Murphy, Director, Institute for Urban Studies at the University of Maryland, College Park (on leave) and Director of the Federal Executive Institute, Charlottesville, Virginia

Also in this series:

SUBURBIA—*Edited by Joseph Zikmund II and Deborah Ellis Dennis*

URBAN COMMUNITY—*Edited by Anthony J. Filipovitch and Earl J. Reeves*

URBAN DECISION MAKING: THE BASIS FOR ANALYSIS—*Edited by Mark Drucker**

URBAN EDUCATION—*Edited by George E. Spear and Donald W. Mocker*

URBAN FISCAL POLICY AND ADMINISTRATION—*Edited by John L. Mikesell and Jerry L. McCaffery**

URBAN HOUSING: PUBLIC AND PRIVATE—*Edited by John E. Rouse, Jr.*

URBAN INDICATORS—*Edited by Thomas P. Murphy**

URBAN LAW—*Edited by Thomas P. Murphy**

URBAN MANAGEMENT—*Edited by Bernard H. Ross*

URBAN POLICY—*Edited by Dennis J. Palumbo and George Taylor*

URBAN POLITICS—*Edited by Thomas P. Murphy*

WOMEN AND URBAN SOCIETY—*Edited by Hasia R. Diner*

*in preparation

The above series is part of the
GALE INFORMATION GUIDE LIBRARY

The Library consists of a number of separate series of guides covering major areas in the social sciences, humanities, and current affairs.

General Editor: Paul Wasserman, Professor and former Dean, School of Library and Information Services, University of Maryland

Managing Editor: Denise Allard Adzigian, Gale Research Company

Urban Planning

A GUIDE TO INFORMATION SOURCES

Volume 2 in the Urban Studies Information Guide Series

Ernest R. Alexander

Associate Professor
Department of Urban Planning
University of Wisconsin-Milwaukee

Anthony James Catanese

Dean and Professor
Department of Urban Planning
University of Wisconsin-Milwaukee

David S. Sawicki

Associate Professor
Department of Urban Planning
University of Wisconsin-Milwaukee

Gale Research Company
Book Tower, Detroit, Michigan 48226

52444

Library of Congress Cataloging in Publication Data

Alexander, Ernest R
    Urban planning.

    (Urban studies information guide series ; v. 2)
    Includes indexes.
    1. City planning—Bibliography. I. Catanese,
Anthony James., joint author. II. Sawicki, David S.,
joint author. III. Title. IV. Series.
Z5942.C37   [HT166]   016.3092'62   78-13462
ISBN 0-8103-1399-5

VITAE

Ernest R. Alexander is associate professor of urban planning at the University of Wisconsin-Milwaukee, and a graduate of the University of California-Berkeley. He has practiced architecture and urban planning in Israel, Britain, and Ghana, worked as a senior planner in California, and has been a consultant for the city of Milwaukee and the state of Wisconsin. He is the author of GOING IT ALONE? A CASE STUDY OF PLANNING AND IMPLEMENTATION AT THE LOCAL LEVEL, and of articles in POLICY SCIENCES and the PUBLIC ADMINISTRATION REVIEW. Currently, he is visiting associate professor at the Technion-Israel Institute of Technology, Haifa.

Anthony James Catanese is the dean and professor of urban planning, School of Architecture and Urban Planning, University of Wisconsin-Milwaukee. He has taught previously at the University of Miami and Georgia Institute of Technology, was a visiting professor at the Virginia Polytechnic University and Clark College, and was a senior Fulbright professor at the Pontificia Universidad Javeriana, Bogotá, Colombia. His consulting work has spanned the country from New York to Hawaii, and he worked as senior planner for the state of New Jersey and Middlesex County, New Jersey. His books include: COMPARATIVE CITY PLANNING; PLANNING AND LOCAL POLITICS: IMPOSSIBLE DREAMS; URBAN TRANSPORTATION IN SOUTH FLORIDA; SYSTEMIC PLANNING: THEORY AND APPLICATION; NEW PERSPECTIVES ON URBAN TRANSPORTATION RESEARCH; and SCIENTIFIC METHODS OF URBAN ANALYSIS. He was a member of President Carter's Urban Policy Task Force during the presidential primary and electoral campaign.

David S. Sawicki is an associate professor in the Department of Urban Planning at the University of Wisconsin-Milwaukee. As assistant dean of the School of Architecture from 1971 through 1973, he developed the Department of Urban Planning which he currently chairs. His teaching and research interests are in the areas of planning methods and development planning, and his publications are focused on these topics. He has been a planning consultant for ten years, and is currently serving on a project for the U.S. Agency for International Development in the Philippines. At present he is the review editor of the JOURNAL OF THE AMERICAN INSTITUTE OF PLANNERS.

CONTENTS

52444

Contents

ABBREVIATIONS

AID	Agency for International Development
AIP	American Institute of Planners
ASPO	American Society of Planning Officials
BASS	Bay Area Simulation Study
B/C or C/B	Benefit-Cost Analysis or Cost-Benefit Analysis
CDC	Community Development Corporation
C/E	Cost-Effectiveness Analysis
CLUG	Community Land Use Game
COG	Council of Government
CPL	Council of Planning Libraries
CPM	Critical Path Method
EDP	Electronic Data Processing
EIS	Environmental Impact Statement
GBO	Governor's Branch Offices
HEW	U.S. Department of Health, Education, and Welfare
HUD	U.S. Department of Housing and Urban Development
MIT	Massachusetts Institute of Technology
NASA	National Aeronautics and Space Administration
NEPA	National Environmental Policy Act
O-D	Origin and Destination Study
OECD	Organization for Economic and Cooperative Development
PERT	Program Evaluation Review Technique
PLUM	Projective Land Use Model
PPBS	Planning-Programming-Budgeting Systems
RERC	Real Estate Research Corporation
RFF	Resources for the Future
SMSA	Standard Metropolitan Statistical Area
TOMM	Time Oriented Simulation Model
TVA	Tennessee Valley Authority
USDA	U.S. Department of Agriculture

ACKNOWLEDGMENT

We extend our gratitude to Mary Eichstaedt for her remarkable abilities in producing a neatly finished manuscript, and in coordinating the project.

INTRODUCTION

Urban planning is a profession dedicated to the improvement of the quality of life and environment of major urban regions. While it evolved from such fields as architecture, landscape architecture, civil engineering, and law, today it incorporates many techniques, methods, and contributions from social sciences, administration and management, systems analysis, mathematics and statistics, health sciences, and the arts and humanities as well. It is truly a hybrid profession owing much to other disciplines.

In order to best develop a guide to the literature of urban planning for the Gale series in Urban Studies, we first had to develop a set of rules for inclusion of bibliographic items. This was essential because one could easily develop a bibliography with much overlap with other titles in this series, due to the broad and comprehensive nature of planning. Thus our first rule was to stress the literature of urban planning, which tends to mean large central cities and surrounding hinterlands. This meant that many aspects of national, state, and regional planning were not incorporated. Secondly, we restricted our entries to comprehensive planning, which means integrative and coordinative processes for the entire spectrum of urban activities, rather than functional planning, which means specialized urban activities planning for transportation, health, social welfare, education, and other matters. This tends to give a somewhat physical orientation to our bibliography largely due to the nature of the literature and practice. Thirdly, we sought entries which we collectively judged to be classical or of highest significance in our opinion. We placed a higher priority on books than on monographs, articles, and ephemeral materials.

The result is what we consider to be the first bibliography of inherent literature for urban planning that represents the most significant entries. This is important to note since other bibliographies might have a different purpose. We would argue, for example, that every library collection at universities with quality programs in urban planning should include, or have ready access to, most of the entries in this bibliography. Similarly, institutions, agencies, and individuals seeking a good library collection on urban planning could consult this bibliography.

For simplicity, we have arranged the bibliographic entries in three general groupings. "History and Development" is inclusive of significant entries on both planning history and the development of the profession. "The Theory and Context of Planning" includes the significant works that relate to urban planning as a process directed towards improved decision making in urban areas as well as the governmental and non-governmental contexts of this process. There also is a brief comparative planning section. Finally, the "Methods and Techniques" grouping includes a wide range of entries dealing with the tools of urban planning for both analysis and implementation.

Chapter 1
HISTORY AND DEVELOPMENT

In reviewing the literature on the history and development of urban planning, we had two major concerns. Our first concern was to select carefully from the prodigious and growing field of urban history only those classical and significant works that related urban history to the planning process. Since the planning process itself has changed with time, we had to stress the physical planning and development of urban areas. Having established that, we sought to examine both twentieth-century and pre-twentieth-century urban planning, as well as those works that evaluated such histories. Our second concern was to examine the development of urban planning as a profession. The literature in this area is rather scant and quite diverse. We had to select carefully from the fields of reform and utopian thought as well as professional ideology and rationale. We also examined and selected entries from the literature dealing with professional roles, issues, and education.

Given these concerns, we chose very carefully and selectively in this chapter. It should be noted that there is much ephemera in the professional literature which we sought to minimize in this bibliography. This is due to the relative newness of urban planning as an organized profession. We can date this to have started in 1917 with the founding of the American Institute of Planners. Thus, with a relatively short professional life span, and the flux in the organizational strength, the literature is not impressive--especially when compared with other professions.

1.1 HISTORY

1.1.1 Pre-Twentieth Century

Collins, George R., gen. ed. PLANNING AND CITIES. 10 vols. New York: Braziller, 1968.

> Braziller Series:
>
> Fraser. Village Planning in the Primitive World
> Lampl. Cities and Planning in the Ancient Near East
> Hardy. Urban Planning in Pre-Columbian America

1

Choay. The Modern City--Planning in the 19th Century
Collins. The Modern City--Planning in the 20th Century
Beneulo, Leonardo. The Origins of Modern Town Planning
Morris, E.J. History of Urban Form
Gatanby, Erwin. New Towns, Antiquity to the Present
Cherry. History of Town Planning--British

One of the best histories of the planning and design of cities.
The ten volumes and authors cover the primitive world, ancient
Near East, pre-Columbian America, medieval cities, ancient Greece
and Italy, Renaissance cities, nineteenth-century cities, Socialist
city planning, twentieth-century cities, and military considerations.

Fein, Albert. FREDERICK LAW OLMSTEAD AND THE AMERICAN ENVIRON-
MENTAL TRADITION. New York: Braziller, 1972. xi, 180 p.

Clearly Olmstead (senior in this case) was the singular starting
point for what has become the planning movement in the United
States. Olmstead was applying modern-day concepts of environmental protection and planning in the nineteenth century, and
this excellent book chronicles that effort.

Glaab, Charles N. THE AMERICAN CITY: A DOCUMENTARY HISTORY.
Homewood, Ill.: Dorsey Press, 1963. xiv, 478 p.

An interesting compilation of historical documents that influenced
urban planning in America. The documents deal with both attitudes toward planning and the political and managerial capabilities
needed to control growth. Mostly eighteenth- and nineteenth-
century documents.

Gutkind, E.A. INTERNATIONAL HISTORY OF CITY DEVELOPMENT. 8 vols.
New York: Free Press, 1964-72. xv, 491 p.

Clearly the best history of the development of cities that exists.
Gutkind's death, after he had prepared the sixth volume, limited the
completion of this world history, but his son, G. Gutkind, edited
the last two volumes from notes and other contributions. Regions
covered include Central Europe, Southern Europe, Western Europe,
Alpine and Scandinavia, and Eastern Europe.

Hilberseimer, L. THE NATURE OF CITIES. Chicago: Paul Theobald, 1955.
286 p.

A classic history of the origin, growth, and decline of cities with
emphasis on pattern and form of development. The book is important for American practice because it is especially critical of the
high densities in American central cities.

Mumford, Lewis. THE CITY IN HISTORY. New York: Harcourt, Brace, and
World, 1961. xi, 657 p.

Probably the most thorough and famous history of cities and their planning that we have, told by the master. This book is indispensable for any serious student of cities and their planning and a must for any library dealing with such matters.

Pirenne, Henri. ECONOMIC AND SOCIAL HISTORY OF MEDIEVAL EUROPE. Translated by I.E. Clegg. New York: Harcourt, Brace, 1959. xii, 243 p.

This translation of the classic French work first published in 1933 indicates the high standard that was set for urban history in the early years of the field. The book deals with the economic and social evolution of cities due to the revival of commerce and industrialization between the eighth and fifteenth centuries. The book is essential for understanding urban growth.

Reps, John W. THE MAKING OF URBAN AMERICA: A HISTORY OF CITY PLANNING IN THE UNITED STATES. Princeton, N.J.: Princeton University Press, 1965. xv, 574 p.

One of the classic books of recent years to analyze the plans and processes that affected urban development in America. The period from colonization by Europeans through the First World War is covered.

Sjoberg, Gideon. THE PRE-INDUSTRIAL CITY. New York: Free Press, 1960. 353 p.

Clearly one of the best reviews of the pre-twentieth-century city with an orientation to the entry-level student in urban affairs or planning. The author covers much of the method and vocabulary of urban history, yet he keeps the book interesting. A global view of early cities is afforded which helps to understand their economy, politics, social base, and physical structure.

Wade, Richard C. THE URBAN FRONTIER: THE RISE OF WESTERN CITIES, 1790-1830. Chicago: University of Chicago Press, 1964. 362 p.

The "western" cities in this case are Cincinnati, Louisville, Lexington, Pittsburgh, and St. Louis during the heyday of the United States' emergence as a nation. The book deals with these early efforts at planning and the first real control of development in the country.

1.1.2 Twentieth Century

Adams, Thomas. OUTLINE OF TOWN AND CITY PLANNING. New York: Russell Sage Foundation, 1935. 368 p.

One of the important historical works on planning, this book provides an overview of the antecedents of urban planning. The book still provides some original materials that are relevant to modern practice. It is very difficult to find this book.

Bender, Thomas. TOWARD AN URBAN VISION: IDEAS AND INSTITUTIONS IN NINETEENTH CENTURY AMERICA. Lexington: University of Kentucky Press, 1975. xv, 277 p.

> An interesting attempt to offer a different perspective to the now-familiar theory of intellectual antagonism to urbanization in America. The author relies heavily on the work of C.C. Brace and F.L. Olmstead as exemplars of making cities fit places in which to live on social and physical terms.

Gallion, Arthur B., and Eisner, Simon. THE URBAN PATTERN. Princeton, N.J.: Van Nostrand, 1963. x, 435 p.

> One of the classic textbooks dealing with urban form. The book is oriented towards the physical form of cities and urban design concepts. It provides a good history of the physical form of cities.

Gelfand, Mark I. A NATION OF CITIES. New York: Oxford University Press, 1975. xvi, 476 p.

> This book analyzes the growth of federal involvement in urban problems during the 1933-65 period. It is especially interesting history in that it deals with both agencies and the personalities that shaped them. The work shows that federal support of cities has been cyclical.

Golany, Gideon, and Waldon, David, eds. THE CONTEMPORARY NEW COMMUNITIES MOVEMENT IN THE UNITED STATES. Urbana: University of Illinois Press, 1975. xiv, 154 p.

> The editors bring together a substantial group of academics and officials in order to evaluate the recent history of the new towns and planned communities movement in America. These evaluations place the movement within a larger societal context which makes it worthwhile.

Gottmann, Jean. MEGALOPOLIS. Cambridge: MIT Press, 1961. xi, 810 p.

> An all-time high in urban analysis in the form of this massive treatment of the 38-million population area of the northeastern United States. Gottmann spent twenty years assembling and analyzing data to create this work. It is at best a reference, but it also presents new concepts of large-area history and evaluation.

Scott, Mel. AMERICAN CITY PLANNING: SINCE 1890. Berkeley and Los Angeles: University of California Press, 1969. xxii, 745 p.

> Commissioned by the American Institute of Planners on the occasion of its fiftieth anniversary, this is the best history of the planning profession in America to appear. The strength of this book

is especially good for the 1890-1940 period wherein much precedent was established. Full of facts and people.

Tunnard, Christopher, and Reed, Henry Hope. AMERICAN SKYLINE: THE GROWTH AND FORM OF OUR CITIES AND TOWNS. Boston: Houghton-Mifflin, 1955. 302 p.

Still the classic popular treatment of the architectural styles and urban design aspects of urban planning history. The book deals primarily with the evolution of urban form rather than socioeconomic trends and influences.

U.S. National Resources Committee. OUR CITIES: THEIR ROLE IN THE NATIONAL ECONOMY. Washington, D.C.: Government Printing Office, 1937. 35 p.

Extremely difficult to find, this study was the landmark official history of U.S. planning for cities. It traces both the planning movement and reform efforts to make cities well-managed and designed. It is rhetorical on the economic significance of cities and planning.

1.1.3 Evaluations of History

Adams, Thomas. OUTLINE OF TOWN AND CITY PLANNING. New York: Russell Sage Foundation, 1935. 368 p.

A rare book that transcends its time and becomes a classic in the field. Adams saw city planning as a unified art with a scientific basis. He details the physical form and patterns of cities from ancient times to early-twentieth century and concludes with lessons to be learned. An excellent book but hard to find.

Anderson, Martin. THE FEDERAL BULLDOZER. Cambridge: MIT Press, 1964. xiv, 272 p.

A critical, sometimes vicious, analysis of the Urban Renewal Program from 1949-62. The book played a major part in the decline of the urban renewal movement by arming its many critics with dubious but effective statistics of program failure.

Bacon, Edmund N. DESIGN OF CITIES. New York: Viking Press, 1967. 296 p.

While a generally good history of the historical evolution of design concepts for cities, this book is excellent as a case study. The city of Philadelphia is used as an example of how design concepts formed the essence of the planning program and gave it form and pattern.

History and Development

Banfield, Edward C. THE UNHEAVENLY CITY. Boston: Little, Brown, 1970. viii, 308 p.

This major book put forward the argument that cities were not as bad as they seemed and most federal programs were making them worse. The argument is based on the premise that historical class differences were at fault rather than race, economics, or housing.

Downs, Anthony. URBAN PROBLEMS AND PROSPECTS. Chicago: Markham, 1970. 293 p.

A series of important articles that Downs had written for a number of journals over an eight-year period. This is an important book because of the unorthodoxy inherent in many of his concepts. Downs ranges from the conservative on urban growth to the radical on transportation to the pragmatist on ghetto development.

Goodman, William I., and Freund, Eric C., eds. PRINCIPLES AND PRACTICE OF URBAN PLANNING. Washington, D.C.: International City Management Association, 1968. 621 p.

This book is as close as anything to a textbook for professional planning practice. It presents basic principles of planning and needed studies. There is an excellent section on planning history, although the implementation section is only fair. A basic part of any library.

Haar, Charles M. BETWEEN THE IDEA AND THE REALITY. A STUDY OF THE ORIGIN, FATE, AND LEGACY OF THE MODEL CITIES PROGRAM. Boston: Little, Brown, 1975. 359 p.

Haar served as an insider in the Johnson administration and uses this book to explain what was right and wrong with the Model Cities program during the mid- to late-sixties. This rare evaluation of recent history by a participant-observer concludes with a proposal for a future national goals survey.

Harrison, Bennett. URBAN ECONOMIC DEVELOPMENT. Washington, D.C.: Urban Institute, 1974. 200 p.

This is a very good evaluation of the changing location of economic activities in the city with special attention being paid to the decentralization of jobs. The evaluation of historical trends concludes that despite all of the suburban development, most jobs are still in the largest cities.

Hawley, Amos H., and Rock, Vincent P., eds. METROPOLITAN AMERICA IN CONTEMPORARY PERSPECTIVE. New York: Wiley, 1975. 504 p.

Another book of readings on the contemporary set of urban problems, but a cut above the average due to the tight editorship and organization. The readings cover a remarkable breadth of social science literature and state of knowledge to evaluate where we are.

Jacobs, Jane. THE ECONOMY OF CITIES. New York: Random House, 1969. 268 p.

A curious, imperfect but interesting theory of how cities first developed and then flourished and fell. The economic aspects are not discussed in technical terms but are argued in didactic terms. Implications for future cities are drawn.

Lynch, Kevin. THE IMAGE OF THE CITY. Cambridge: MIT Press, 1960. 194 p.

This book is a basic source for perception and understanding of urban design. Yet beyond the techniques, tools, and terminology, Lynch has contributed something more lasting, an entirely new way of thinking about and looking at cities. Since there are many titles on this subject, it is noteworthy that a single book could do this.

Moynihan, Daniel P. MAXIMUM FEASIBLE MISUNDERSTANDING. New York: Free Press, 1969. xxi, 218 p.

An analysis of the frustrations, failures, and ultimate violence that resulted from the well-intended but misunderstood role of citizens in the planning process. The experiences are drawn largely from the War on Poverty during the late 1960s as part of Lyndon Johnson's ambitious program.

Mumford, Lewis. THE URBAN PROSPECT. New York: Harcourt, Brace, and World, 1968. xx, 255 p.

Of Mumford's many writings, this group of articles is especially important for urban planning. He sets forth his prescriptions for planning which tend to be heavily based upon new town and regional dispersal. He sees these as the basis for practice.

Perloff, Harvey [S.], et al. MODERNIZING THE CENTRAL CITY. Cambridge, Mass.: Ballinger, 1975. xxx, 414 p.

Results of a large research project that examined how central cities could be modernized, especially through the so-called "new town-in town" approach. The results also include case studies from New York, Boston, San Antonio, and several other major projects.

Redstone, Louis G. THE NEW DOWNTOWNS. New York: McGraw-Hill, 1976. 330 p.

This compendium of case studies deals with the contemporary practice and success with downtown recycling and renovation. It is a well-illustrated book with many plans and drawings of interest to both designer and planner.

Sternlieb, George, and Hughes, James W., eds. POST-INDUSTRIAL AMERI-
CA: METROPOLITAN DECLINE AND INTER-REGIONAL JOB SHIFTS. New
Brunswick, N.J.: Rutgers University, 1975. 267 p.

> A group of essays dealing with recent trends in the metropolitan
> and national structure of homes and jobs. The essays deal primarily
> with the decline of older urban centers and the growth of the sun-
> belt urban areas. There is some prophetic futures analysis.

Tunnard, Christopher, and Pushkarev, Boris. MAN-MADE AMERICA: CHAOS
OR CONTROL? New Haven, Conn.: Yale University Press, 1963. xii,
479 p.

> A good contemporary history of urban America, this well-known
> book is also a valuable source for practice. It is oriented toward
> the esthetics of cities and discusses the needs for a better integra-
> tion of design and planning to control the form of cities.

Walker, Robert A. THE PLANNING FUNCTION IN URBAN GOVERNMENT.
2d ed. Chicago: University of Chicago Press, 1950. 410 p.

> This book was far ahead of its time in proposing planning as a
> function of the executive branch to advise on policy and manage
> growth. The book also includes a detailed history of planning
> from 1900 to the 1930s, with a heavy concentration on land use
> and zoning.

1.2 DEVELOPMENT OF PROFESSION

1.2.1 Reform and Utopian Thought

Eldredge, H. Wentworth, ed. TAMING MEGALOPOLIS. 2 vols. New York:
Praeger, 1967. xv, 1,166 p.

> A large group of readings that gives a good overview to most prob-
> lems of contemporary urban planning for the large cities and re-
> gions of the United States. There are many readings dealing with
> principles and theories of modern planning practice. Several read-
> ings deal with the historical evolution of problems.

Forrester, Jay W. URBAN DYNAMICS. Cambridge: MIT Press, 1969. xiii,
285 p.

> The hallmark of the systems approach movement in urban planning.
> This book argues that cities can be viewed as open systems and
> planned accordingly. The concept of the counter-intuitive rule
> is introduced which argues that planners should reject the obvious.

Howard, Ebenezer. GARDEN CITIES OF TO-MORROW. Cambridge: MIT
Press, 1965. 168 p.

A recent edition of the classic 1898 book--originally called TO-
MORROW: A PEACEFUL PATH TO REAL REFORM by Howard--
with a preface by F.Y. Osborn. Not only are the original plans
for garden cities included, but also there are a very good essay
by Lewis Mumford on modern relevance of the concepts and a
fine book list.

LaPatra, Jack [W.]. APPLYING THE SYSTEMS APPROACH TO URBAN DEVELOP-
MENT. Stroudsburg, Pa.: Dowden, Hutchinson, and Ross, 1975. ix, 296 p.

There have been a number of books addressed toward this subject,
but this is the only one that attempts to reach a nontechnical
audience. As a result, it borders on polemic and proselytizing
at times. Its value is for the nonspecialist interested in a general understanding of what system analysis is and can be in urban
planning.

Moynihan, Daniel P., ed. TOWARD A NATIONAL URBAN POLICY. New
York: Basic Books, 1970. xiv, 348 p.

An important effort to sketch the elements of what the federal
role should be in urban affairs and planning. Most of the articles
predictably argue for more money and research, but Moynihan's
piece is special. He argues for a federal policy of population
group and social group location.

Reiner, Thomas A. THE PLACE OF THE IDEAL COMMUNITY IN URBAN
PLANNING. Philadelphia: University of Pennsylvania Press, 1963. 194 p.

The best serious compilation and analysis of the utopian schemes
and plans for cities. The author develops an excellent format and
content analysis to compare the major utopian designs and how
they emerged over time. A unique contemporary history as well.

Woods, Shadrach. THE MAN IN THE STREET. Baltimore, Md.: Penguin,
1975. 234 p.

A polemic of some interest on the evolution of urban regions and
the problems they have generated. The proposed solution is to
plan for urban growth on a regional scale including population,
buildings, and environment. The author was a disciple of Le Cor-
busier.

1.2.2 Ideology and Rationale

Branch, Melville C. PLANNING: ASPECTS AND APPLICATIONS. New
York: Wiley, 1966. 333 p.

This book is a compilation of Branch's theories of planning practice
and process as a comprehensive undertaking. He foresees the day
when all forms of planning, public, private, and military, will

require a new professional trained in comprehensive rather than functional planning.

Doxiadis, Constantinos A. EKISTICS: AN INTRODUCTION TO THE SCIENCE OF HUMAN SETTLEMENTS. London: Hutchinson, 1968. xxix, 527 p.

> Most likely the single, most important writing of the late Doxiadis. This book is a very detailed submission of his case for an integrated study of urbanization and development through a multidisciplinary set of principles and techniques that he called "Ekistics." The major contribution of this book is the scope and breadth of the concepts.

Erber, Ernest, ed. URBAN PLANNING IN TRANSITION. New York: Grossman, 1970. xxviii, 323 p.

> This book is the result of an important conference that dealt with the ideology and theory of planning practice. Such topics as planning in its societal framework, the state of the art, and the role of professional planners are well covered.

Friedan, Bernard J., and Morris, Robert, eds. URBAN PLANNING AND SOCIAL POLICY. New York: Basic Books, 1968. xvii, 459 p. Paperbound.

> An important book of readings which attempts to relate the profession and practice of urban planning to the social policy issues and problems. Most of these issues are particular to the large cities of the East Coast but tend to be not really regional.

Friedmann, John. RETRACKING AMERICA: A THEORY OF TRANSACTIVE PLANNING. Garden City, N.Y.: Anchor Press, 1973. xx, 289 p.

> While a paean to the "I plan O.K., you plan O.K." school of professionalism, and a rather cumbersome and impractical theory of practice, it is one of the few books to place planning practice in a societal-knowing context. The author owes much to Karl Mannheim and, perhaps, Plato.

Friedmann, John, and Alonso, William, eds. REGIONAL DEVELOPMENT AND PLANNING. Cambridge: MIT Press, 1964. xiii, 722 p.

> The best single collection of the important articles and summaries of the regional planning movement from the analytical side. The readings are largely historical pieces that were influential in forming the present body of knowledge.

_____. REGIONAL POLICY: READINGS IN THEORY AND APPLICATIONS. Cambridge: MIT Press, 1975. 808 p.

> A massive collection of readings on the theory and applications of large-scale, regional policy. This is essentially an update and

expansion of Friedmann's and Alonso's REGIONAL DEVELOPMENT
AND PLANNING (above), yet it contains very few of the "classic"
essays.

Kulski, Julian. LAND OF URBAN PROMISE. Notre Dame, Ind.: University
of Notre Dame Press, 1967. xx, 282 p.

A history of the design and planning of northeastern United States
also contains an ideology. The author argues that there has been
a great tradition of planning and design in this part of the United
States and planning for the future megalopolis should be rooted in
greatness.

MacKaye, Benton. THE NEW EXPLORATION: A PHILOSOPHY OF REGIONAL
PLANNING. (With introduction by Lewis Mumford.) Urbana: University of
Illinois Press, 1962. 243 p.

This version of the 1928 classic includes an introduction that describes the work as "pioneering" and "ahead of much of the thinking and planning being done today." There is much truth in that
commentary. MacKaye's concepts of regionalism, environmental
protection, development, and growth control continue to be fascinating and worthwhile reading.

Mayer, R.; Moroney, R.; and Morris, R[obert]. CENTRALLY PLANNED CHANGE.
Urbana: University of Illinois Press, 1975. viii, 230 p.

This book is a reexamination of the theory and practice of urban
development planning for social issues such as health and employment. The book covers theoretical bases for planning to a major
extent and includes disciplinary perspectives.

Moore, Gary T., and Golledge, Reginald D., eds. ENVIRONMENTAL
KNOWING. Stroudsburg, Pa.: Dowden, Hutchinson, and Ross, 1976.
441 p.

This book is an important work in the area of environment-behavior
studies. It deals with issues of interchange and interaction of
people with their built and natural surroundings. As such, it introduces critical new perspectives for design and planning that had
been previously ignored or left to chance. While a research orientation is proffered, there is much subjectivity.

Schnore, Leo F., and Fagin, Henry, eds. URBAN RESEARCH AND POLICY
PLANNING. Beverly Hills, Calif.: Sage, 1967. 638 p.

An important book of readings which helped establish much contemporary theory and practice for planning. The essence of the
book is to show that social issues are the most critical for planners, and they should shift practice away from physical design to
policy coordination.

1.2.3 Professional Issues and Development

American Institute of Planners. "Code of Professional Responsibility and Rules of Procedure." 1976 ROSTER, pp. iv–v. Washington, D.C.: 1976. vii, 168 p.

> This is the only evidence to suggest that there are any standards of ethical practice for the planning profession. These ethics are divided into "canons," which are pompous-sounding and rhetorical, and "rules of procedure," which seem more directed toward client relations and how to do business. These standards raise serious doubts about the credibility of ethical commitments.

_____. THE SOCIAL RESPONSIBILITY OF THE PLANNER. Washington, D.C.: 1973. 8 p.

> An expansion of the guidelines that are recommended for planners seeking to fulfill the AIP canons on ethics that state each planner shall seek to increase choices available to people, especially those with the least ability to choose. The statement is wordy and vague and involves no apparent sanctions. Some of the guidelines are silly since they imply decisions that are societal rather than professional.

Bair, Frederick H. PLANNING CITIES. Chicago: American Society of Planning Officials, 1970. xi, 499 p.

> The iconoclast par excellence of planning sets forth his experiential wisdom of practice in this book. Besides being witty and often tongue-in-cheek, Bair provides insights that can only be gained by years of professional practice and too easily dismissed in a book.

Black, Russell Van Nest. PLANNING AND THE PLANNING PROFESSION. Washington, D.C.: American Institute of Planners, 1967. xiv, 64 p.

> A historical review of the development of the planning profession during 1917–67. It traces the people, places, and events that were significant and provides interesting vignettes of the major professional planners of the period. It was commissioned for the fiftieth anniversary of AIP.

Catanese, Anthony James. "Credentials and Certification of Planners." PRACTICING PLANNER 2 (October 1976): 8–11.

> A proposal and rationale for avoiding state-by-state licensing and registration of professional planners by developing a national body charged with certifying the competency of planners. The controversial idea would issue a certification based upon education, experience, and testing.

_____. LICENSING AND REGISTRATION OF PROFESSIONAL PLANNERS: THE COMING ISSUE. Washington, D.C.: American Institute of Planners, 1975. 16 p.

> An analysis and evaluation of the state efforts to license and regis-
> ter professional planners. Only New Jersey licenses planners and
> only Michigan registers planners by title. The author examines
> the financial, political, and social issues of licensing and registra-
> tion and recommends that a national standard of certification be
> developed.

Chapin, F. Stuart, Jr. URBAN LAND USE PLANNING. 2d ed. Urbana: University of Illinois Press, 1965. xvi, 498 p.

> There never has been and never will be a better book on how to
> do land use planning for small and medium cities. Chapin's book,
> despite its age, is essential for any practitioner. He covers all
> the techniques that are basic and offers some surprising new ap-
> proaches.

Goodman, Robert. AFTER THE PLANNERS. New York: Simon and Schuster, 1971. 231 p.

> A vituperative, vitriolic, and downright nasty polemical attack on
> architecture and planning which the author sees as reason that
> radical change is not occurring in cities. Beyond this silly prem-
> ise, the author does offer some interesting experiences on plan-
> ning failures but provides no answers.

Marcuse, Peter. "Professional Ethics and Beyond: Values in Planning." JOURNAL OF AMERICAN INSTITUTE OF PLANNERS 42 (July 1976): 264-75.

> Incredibly this is probably the only serious discussion of the ethics
> of professional planners. Yet the title implies the weakness of
> the argument. The author does not see ethics as distinct from
> value judgments and argues that values are more important than
> ethical standards. This may be the case for a loosely organized
> profession, but it could hardly stand the test in medicine or law.
> Worth reading because of uniqueness.

1.2.4 Professional Roles

Altshuler, Alan. THE CITY PLANNING PROCESS: A POLITICAL ANALY-SIS. Ithaca, N.Y.: Cornell University Press, 1965. x, 466 p.

> One of the first serious analyses of the flaws in the planning pro-
> cess as a technical endeavor within a political arena. The case
> studies in the book point to many problems that inhibit the imple-
> mentation of planning recommendations.

Beyle, T.L., and Lathrop, G.T., eds. PLANNING AND POLITICS: UNEASY
PARTNERSHIP. New York: Odyssey, 1970. x, 277 p.

A very interesting collection of readings that explores planning
within a political framework. Such aspects as technique, style,
and approach are covered. The authors also explore political
ideology as a factor to be dealt with by planners. More of the
latter should have been developed.

Bolan, Richard S., and Nuttall, Ronald L. URBAN PLANNING AND POLI-
TICS. Lexington, Mass.: D.C. Heath, 1975. xviii, 211 p.

An empirical testing of a rather complicated theory of how the
planning process should work in political life. There are numerous
case studies that show clear evidence of a breakdown in the process and structure of planning in large cities that seems to prevent
implementation.

Catanese, Anthony J[ames]. PLANNERS AND LOCAL POLITICS: IMPOSSIBLE
DREAMS. Beverly Hills, Calif.: Sage, 1974. 189 p.

A well-known analysis of the political basis for planning failures
in the United States. The argument is made that changes are necessary in the planning 'process and ideology if we are to expect
implementation of planning. There are discussions of the planning
process also.

Rabinovitz, Francine F. CITY POLITICS AND PLANNING. New York:
Atherton Press, 1969. 200 p.

An analysis of the role of the planner in the local political system.
It is highly critical of the practice of planning in that it does not
relate well to that process. There is little in the way of suggested
improvements, however.

Rondinelli, Dennis A. URBAN AND REGIONAL DEVELOPMENT PLANNING:
POLICY AND ADMINISTRATION. Ithaca, N.Y.: Cornell University Press,
1975. 272 p.

This book has two parts. The first part is a major review of the
political, technical, and theoretical issues of professional planning
as a process and career. This evaluation makes significant observa-
tions and recommends solutions. The second part is a less satisfy-
ing case study of regional economic development in Appalachia.

Spreiregen, Paul D. URBAN DESIGN: THE ARCHITECTURE OF TOWNS AND
CITIES. New York: McGraw-Hill, 1965. xi, 243 p.

An ambitious effort to chronicle the emergence of urban design in
America and develop a process and role in the planning process.
It is more substantive than similar books and should be useful to
architects trying to define their role in the urban planning process.

1.2.5 Professional Education

Adams, Frederick. URBAN PLANNING EDUCATION IN THE UNITED STATES. Cincinnati: Alfred Bettman Foundation, 1954. v, 180 p.

While the currency of the program offerings seriously limits the usefulness of this book, its evaluative part is of much greater value. This was the first major effort to evaluate planning education and as such deals with issues of degrees, curriculum, and philosophy that are yet to be resolved.

Catanese, Anthony J[ames]. "Doctor of Planning: A Degree Proposal for Further Consideration." BULLETIN OF THE ASSOCIATION OF COLLEGIATE SCHOOLS OF PLANNING 7 (Winter 1969): 5-10.

An argument for a new, higher-order degree for professional planners. Catanese says that the bachelor and master level degrees do not provide sufficient coverage of the technical and procedural aspects of planning needed for sophisticated areas such as state and regional planning. He also sees the need for a structured residency required prior to graduation.

_____. "Quo Vadis, Planning Education." BULLETIN OF THE ASSOCIATION OF COLLEGIATE SCHOOLS OF PLANNING 8 (Winter 1970): 7-9.

A brief discussion of the trends in planning education from the viewpoint of graduate professional work. Catanese sees the need for new approaches and new degrees.

Godschalk, David R., ed. PLANNING IN AMERICA: LEARNING FROM TURBULENCE. Washington, D.C.: American Institute of Planners, 1974. 229 p.

An interesting collection of articles which attempts to evaluate recent urban history in order to improve planning education. Despite the somewhat overplayed notion of turbulence in cities, there are important contributions made to the context of urban planning although the substance is vague.

Perloff, Harvey S. EDUCATION FOR PLANNING: CITY, STATE, AND REGIONAL. Baltimore, Md.: Johns Hopkins Press, 1957. 189 p.

While known widely as the classic work on education for professional planners, Perloff's book provides an excellent history of the planning movement in America from 1893 to 1955. This is done by a detailed chronology of major planning events.

Susskind, Lawrence, ed. GUIDE TO GRADUATE EDUCATION IN URBAN AND REGIONAL PLANNING. East Lansing, Mich.: Association of Collegiate Schools of Planning, 1974. 304 p.

History and Development

This monograph was intended to serve as both a guide to prospective students and an evaluation of various programs. The guide portion is of value to students and others interested in planning education. The qualitative appraisal, based upon questionnaire responses, is somewhat dubious and not as valuable. The 1977 edition is edited by Michael Brooks and turns the qualitative analysis over to the schools themselves.

Chapter 2

THE THEORY AND CONTEXT OF PLANNING

In reviewing the literature on the theory and context of planning, we are using the term "planning" in its widest sense. In this sense, planning is regarded as "a process for determining future action through a sequence of choices" (David-off and Reiner, 1962), or "the attempt to control the consequences of our ac-tions" (Wildavsky, 1973). This approach raises the problem of possible overlap with cognate fields such as policy, administration, and management, a prob-lem we are prepared to accept.

The other alternative--a narrow definition of planning as limited to planned in-tervention in the physical urban environment--would allot to planning only activities ranging from municipal engineering to land-use control. This defini-tion is today accepted neither by practitioners of planning, nor by students or theorists in the field, as the references throughout this volume show.

A broad approach to planning has the advantage, too, of allowing us to tap the roots of planning-theory literature in decision theory, organization theory, and political, social, and economic theory, roots which planning has in common with the aforementioned related areas. The problem of overlap with policy making, administration, and management is addressed by entering those references which are basic and common to all these fields but omitting the more special-ized literature which is particular to the nonplanning areas.

Two other problems must be confronted which are peculiar to the literature covered in this chapter. One problem is the number of important references which are in the form of journal articles. This has led us to depart from the emphasis on monograph publications which is our policy in the other parts of this book. The market for planning theory-oriented books, apparently, is more limited than for books with a historical or a methodological orientation. The other problem is how to deal with references contained in anthologies. This is the case with several articles referenced in this chapter which appear in anthologies whose titles give no hint of their actual contents. As a result we decided, in the interests of clarity and easier retrieval, to enter such articles under their own authors and titles, even when that requires multiple entry of the same anthology which may contain more than one such reference.

Theory and Context of Planning

The overall structure of this chapter is suggested by the title. The first section, "Planning Theory," covers the literature dealing with the rationale for planning activity, its background in decision theory, and general descriptions of planning models, processes, and roles. The following sections all relate planning to a particular context in which it is carried out, and are organized to reflect the range of different planning environments which exist and which are covered in the literature.

The organization of the first section was determined by two factors: one was a deliberate conceptual rationale; the other emerged from the literature itself. The conceptual organizational framework suggested three headings. One would cover the rationale for planning: the "why" of the planning activity in general, of planned public intervention, and of the planning profession in particular. The second would cover the roots of planning in individual and organizational decision making, without which much of the "how" of planning cannot be understood. The third would address planning theory itself: the "what is it" and "how does it happen" of planning.

Two of these headings indeed remained untouched through the editorial process, and this chapter begins with "Individual and Organizational Decision Making" and "The Rationale for Planning." The third heading proved too cumbersome to stay undivided, and the classifications of its titles were suggested by the broad groupings of the references themselves.

While many of these references cover more than one of the areas suggested in the section headings, they are located according to what seems to be their major emphasis. Titles where the focus is on a more abstract description or definition of planning, or which propose or describe particular models of planning whose context is secondary, are listed under "Planning Theory and Models." Other references, with a more concrete orientation, often with specific contexts and cases, fall under "Process, Context, and Roles." Finally, a heading was assigned to a number of titles which addressed planning more from its ideological aspects or with a normative focus on planning for a changing society.

It is in the nature of this type of literature not to have a clearly defined or delimited content. Consequently many of the aforementioned classifications will be to some extent subjective or arbitrary, and it would certainly be difficult for the reader to know, by its title alone, under which heading to find a particular reference. While we have used cross-referencing elsewhere to identify works bridging between areas, we have not done so here, as it would have led to substantial duplication. Where any doubt exists as to the substantive classification of a particular title, therefore, the reader is advised to refer to all three of these headings.

The next two sections cover the various contexts of planning. As this volume is designed primarily for the American reader, these sections restrict their coverage to the United States. The headings in the section, "The Governmental Context," reflect the various levels of government in which planning takes place, which also correspond to a range of scales of areal units of concern.

In this section, too, there is some overlap, not because of conceptual vagueness this time but because some works address more than a single level of government. Regional planning problems, for example, are frequently addressed in the context of state government, on the one hand, or of metropolitan regions, on the other. Where a work offers significant coverage under more than one heading, it is also cross-referenced under its second theme.

Unlike all prior bibliographies on planning in various levels of government, we have excluded from the following references any titles of government-originated ephemera. This includes policy documents, plans, studies, and reports, unless they have been reissued in the form of books or (rarely) journal articles. This literature is vast, and it is expanding exponentially day by day. But we believe that it is only of limited interest to the nonspecialized reader, and that the usefulness of including such references even for the specialized researcher is obviated by their extremely rapid obsolescence.

"Non-Governmental Planning" includes two quite unrelated headings, which have in common only that they represent contexts for planning outside the various levels of general and special purpose government. Planning in the private sector is an extensive activity, and its impact on American society, if Kenneth Galbraith is to be believed, can hardly be underestimated. This importance, however, bears no relation to the extent of its literature, which after somewhat of a flowering in the early sixties has been sparse indeed.

The scarcity of references to corporate planning may perhaps be accentuated by our criteria of selection. We have restricted the titles included here to those dealing with corporate planning as a comprehensive activity, and primarily descriptive. This has resulted in the exclusion of many titles dealing normatively (such as, in a "how to" sense) with sectoral planning related activities in corporate management, such as market projection, and investment analysis.

In referencing titles under "Neighborhood and Community," we have also attempted to be selective, focussing on references which have planning as one of their central themes. The literature on neighborhood and community planning expands almost imperceptibly into areas such as citizen participation, community government, community development organizations, neighborhood politics, and the like. Titles with any of these themes as their exclusive focus have been omitted, but many neighborhood and community planning issues have been addressed in the context of one or more of these themes. Where such a work includes substantial content of planning interest, therefore, it has been included.

A final section gives a sampling of the literature addressing planning outside the United States. This literature is also extensive, but titles have been selected with several considerations in mind. To be included here, references had to be of general interest and intelligible to a reader unfamiliar with the foreign context. The focus was to be mainly on planning in the general şense and not on a specific sectoral aspect alone. And, finally, the work was to have primarily a descriptive orientation, rather than instructing the reader on how to grapple with the problem of planning in strange contexts and societies.

Given these constraints, we feel that the inclusion of a section on planning outside the United States, and of studies comparing American planning with other planning efforts, is worthwhile. Though the focus of this volume is on planning in the United States, it is important to put American planning into its wider context, if only to realize to what extent it has been shaped by the particular characteristics of this policy and society.

2.1 BACKGROUND AND RATIONALE

2.1.1 Individual and Organizational Decision Making

Alexander, Christopher. NOTES ON THE SYNTHESIS OF FORM. Cambridge, Mass.: Harvard University Press, 1964. 216 p.

> In this analysis of the problem-solving process, Alexander conceptualizes design as a cumulative process of incremental solutions leading to system-wide redesign. A novel approach applying systems concepts to design and creativity.

Alexander, Ernest R. "Choice in a Changing World." POLICY SCIENCES 3 (September 1972): 325-37.

> A critique of general theories of decision making which are not related to the decision context. Two alternative models of decision making are suggested, which depend on the decision makers' perceived environment.

Bower, Joseph L. "Descriptive Decision Theory from the Administrative Viewpoint." In THE STUDY OF POLICY FORMATION, edited by Raymond A. Bauer and Kenneth J. Gergen, pp. 103-48. New York: Free Press, 1968.

> A well-organized and concise review of descriptive decision theory, organization theory, and political theory as they bear on administrative decision making. The survey begins with basic economic decision theory and ranges through the experimental psychologists (Edwards, Coombs, Siegel), the Carnegie school of organizational behavior (March, Newell, Simon), econometrics, organizational sociology (Barnard, Selznick, Thompson), the experimental economists and political scientists (Buchanan and Tullock, Downs, Riker, Fouraker) to games theory. The author pleads for a synthesis of normative and descriptive theory and concludes that field research is essential.

Braybrooke, David, and Lindblom, Charles E. A STRATEGY OF DECISION: POLICY EVALUATION AS A SOCIAL PROCESS. Glencoe, Ill.: Free Press, 1963. ix, 268 p.

In this work, which blends the normative with the descriptive, the authors attack the rational-deductive ideal as a decision-making model for its claim to separate factual and value elements and its aspiration to comprehensiveness. They propose the strategy of "disjointed incrementalism" as a more realistic and better way to explore the reciprocal relationship between means and ends.

Cohen, Michael D.; March, James G.; and Olsen, Johann P. "A Garbage Can Model of Organizational Choice." ADMINISTRATIVE SCIENCE QUARTER-LY 17 (March 1972): 1-25.

Based on studies and a simulation of organizational decision making in universities, the authors conclude that problem solving is a reciprocal process of mating existing problems with available solutions. The choice opportunity is likened to a "garbage can" into which are dumped the decision outcomes of four independent streams in the organization: problems, solutions, participants, and opportunities. They conclude that this model is effective in enabling some problem resolution, though it does not resolve problems well.

Dyckman, John W. "Planning and Decision Theory." JOURNAL OF AMERICAN INSTITUTE OF PLANNERS 27 (November 1961): 335-45.

Dyckman reviews the development of decision theory and its relevance and application to planning. Included is relevant work to 1960 in probability and welfare economics, experimental psychology, and political and organization theory. The most complete review to date, and one which, unfortunately, has not been subsequently updated by any review of comparable completeness and quality.

Etzioni, Amitai. "Mixed Scanning: A 'Third' Approach to Decision-Making." PUBLIC ADMINISTRATION REVIEW 27 (December 1967): 385-92.

Decision making is related to the degree of control over the situation, with the rational model assuming maximum control and incrementalism very little. Mixed scanning, involving several levels of detail and coverage, is proposed as an intermediate model covering most contexts.

Gamson, William A. "Game Theory and Administrative Decision Making." In EMPATHY AND IDEOLOGY, edited by Charles Press and Alan Arlan, pp. 146-61. Chicago: Rand-McNally, 1966.

A review of game theory and its application to administrative decision making. Its limitations are pointed out: the problem definition is taken as given, as are the goals. Therefore, it is limited to choice between technical alternatives only.

Gore, William J. ADMINISTRATIVE DECISION MAKING: A HEURISTIC
MODEL. New York: Wiley, 1964. 191 p.

> A dynamic model of decision making at local government adminis-
> trative levels is presented. Three types of decisions are identified:
> routine, adaptive, and innovative. The author focuses on the
> distinction between rational-habituated and well-integrated behav-
> ior, and heuristic behavior, incorporating spontaneity and impro-
> visation, which may be more appropriate for indeterminate situa-
> tions.

Gremion, Catherine. "A New Theory of Decision Making?" INTERNATION-
AL STUDIES OF MANAGEMENT AND ORGANIZATION 2 (Summer 1972): 125-
43.

> Existing decision theories are criticized for their divorce from the
> social context of decision making, including the roles of power and
> influence as determinants of outcomes.

Klein, Burton H. "The Decision Making Problem in Development." In THE
RATE AND DIRECTION OF INVENTIVE ACTIVITY, National Bureau of Economic Research, pp. 477-508. Princeton, N.J.: Princeton University Press, 1962.

> An analysis of decision making in weapons research and develop-
> ment. Based on a rate of learning hypothesis, Klein suggests the
> possibility, in certain situations, of pursuing alternative solutions
> simultaneously.

Levin, P.H. "On Decisions and Decision Making." PUBLIC ADMINISTRATION
50 (Spring 1972): 19-44.

> Decisions are identified in terms of commitment and specificity,
> and three types of decision processes--technical, administrative,
> and political--are suggested, which are composed of different
> mixes of these types. The model is applied to analyze three cases
> in Britain.

Lindblom, Charles E. THE INTELLIGENCE OF DEMOCRACY: DECISION
MAKING THROUGH MUTUAL ADJUSTMENT. New York: Free Press, 1965.
viii, 352-p.

> Bargaining is proposed as the central feature of the democratic so-
> cial decision process. A detailed taxonomy of different types of
> bargaining is presented, and bargaining is put into the context of
> incremental decision making. Lindblom emphasizes the advantages
> of this process but concedes that it depends on agreement with
> the existing distribution of authority.

_____. THE POLICY MAKING PROCESS. Englewood Cliffs, N.J.: Pren-
tice-Hall, 1968. vi, 122 p. Paperbound.

> Policy making is related to policy analysis in a sequential decision

process. The author suggests that this approach minimizes risk and keeps options open and is usually adopted for reasons of political feasibility.

Mack, Ruth P. PLANNING ON UNCERTAINTY: DECISION MAKING IN BUSINESS AND GOVERNMENT ADMINISTRATION. New York: Wiley-Interscience, 1971. xi, 233 p.

A comprehensive overview of the ongoing process of administrative decision making. The book contains three parts. In the first part, "Choice by 'Rational' Man," the fundamentals of statistical decision theory are reviewed and some methods are presented. The second part, "Choice by Natural Man," develops a typology of decision situations, focusing on the cost of uncertainty. The third part, "Ongoing Deliberative Processes," puts decision situations into the real life context of ongoing processes.

Miller, George A.; Galanter, Eugene; and Pribram, Karl H. PLANS AND THE STRUCTURE OF BEHAVIOR. New York: Henry Holt, 1960. 226 p.

A psychological presentation of planning as an essential component of behavior, which is disaggregated into TOTE (test-operate-test-execute) units. Plans are related to memory, speech, and problem-solving processes, in an effort to arrive at a synthesis between cognitive and behavioral psychology.

Newell, Alan, and Simon, Herbert A. HUMAN PROBLEM SOLVING. Englewood Cliffs, N.J.: Prentice-Hall, 1972. xiv, 920 p.

The definitive work to date describing the individual approach to complex problems. Summarizing over twenty years' work by the authors, and incorporating new original research on problem-solving situations, such as chess and acrostic puzzles, Newell and Simon see the problem-solving process as a heuristic search and information processing system. This work has important implications for the intelligence and design phases of the planning process.

Olson, Mancur. THE LOGIC OF COLLECTIVE ACTION: PUBLIC GOODS AND THE THEORY OF GROUPS. Cambridge, Mass.: Harvard University Press, 1965. 176 p.

A review of group and organization theories focusing on consensus and bargaining. The labor union, its internal organization and social impact, is analyzed as an empirical example. The author introduces the concept of "by-product" pressure groups which engage in political activity as a secondary function to their main purpose. The thrust of this classic work is highly relevant for planning: that organized groups are the basic unit for the aggregation of public values. Its impact was felt in the development of the pluralist school of public decision making and in the emergence of planning models such as advocacy planning.

Rein, Martin. "Social Policy Analysis as the Interpretation of Beliefs." JOURNAL OF AMERICAN INSTITUTE OF PLANNERS 37 (September 1971): 297-310.

Rein defines social policy as choice among competing values. The translation of values into policy involves beliefs at each level of analysis: in definitions of purpose, in assignment of priorities, in the choice of instrumentalities, and in outcome evaluation. The paper concludes that there is no one true policy analysis, a frustrating stance but perhaps productive for future analysts.

Simon, Herbert A. ADMINISTRATIVE BEHAVIOR: A STUDY OF DECISION-MAKING PROCESSES IN ADMINISTRATIVE ORGANIZATION. 3d ed. New York: Free Press, 1976. 259 p.

The rational decision model is here given extensive formulation from a theoretical and behavioral perspective. Case illustrations are essentially from a managerial-corporate perspective, but of general relevance. In the introduction to this edition Simon introduces his concept of bounded rationality which leads to the "satisfycing" model of decision making referred to here but more fully developed elsewhere.

_____. MODELS OF MAN. New York: Wiley, 1957. 287 p.

In the two essays in this book, Simon lays out one of the most important insights in contemporary descriptive decision theory. The first, "Rationality and the Environment," develops a model of decision behavior in conditions of limited information and resources, based on a heuristic search process. The second, "A Behavioral Model of Rational Choice," contrasts the formal rational model of choice with a more realistic one which, rather than optimizing, constrains the search for solutions to meeting a flexible aspiration level. Together these essays present the decision model which Simon called "satisfycing," which is the basis of much of the subsequent research into decision behavior.

_____. THE SCIENCES OF THE ARTIFICIAL. Cambridge: MIT Press, 1969. 123 p.

Simon develops here the logical link between scientific knowledge and organized action. He explicates the role of design in the decision and problem-solving process in a unique contribution to this extensive literature.

Thompson, James D. ORGANIZATIONS IN ACTION. New York: McGraw-Hill, 1967. xi, 192 p.

Thompson describes how organizational structure and decision behavior is determined by the organization's tasks and its relations to its environment. Of particular interest is his classification of

52444   24

decision types, depending on the decision makers' beliefs about cause-effect relations and their certainty about their outcome preferences.

Vickers, Geoffrey. THE ART OF JUDGMENT: A STUDY OF POLICY MAKING. New York: Basic Books, 1965. 242 p.

Vickers sees policy making as a process combining reality judgments with value judgments. The development of the Buchanan report on transportation policy, the Robbins report on higher education, and the Gowers report on capital punishment are analyzed to illustrate this proposition. The need for adaptive planning is deduced from the effects of societal change on the quality of prediction. Cases of organizational decision making are presented to show how the "appreciative system" applies balancing and optimizing criteria of survival, growth, and efficiency.

Walton, Richard E. "Interorganizational Decision Making and Identity Conflict." In INTERORGANIZATIONAL DECISION MAKING, edited by Matthew Tuite et al., pp. 94-111. Chicago: Aldine, 1972. xvi, 298 p.

Interorganizational relations are analyzed in terms of respective organizations' goals and preferences, and the types of values--instrumental or expressive--which are at stake. This analysis leads to conclusions about the types of situations which elicit avoidance or engagement in joint decision making.

Warren, Roland L.; Rose, Stephen M.; and Bergunder, Ann F. THE STRUCTURE OF URBAN REFORM: COMMUNITY DECISION ORGANIZATIONS IN STABILITY AND CHANGE. Lexington, Mass.: D.C. Heath, 1974. xiii, 220 p.

A survey of Model Cities agencies and other community decision organizations in nine cities provides the context for this conceptualization of organizational decision behavior and interorganizational relations. In contrast to prior models focused on a central organization, this model is based on an interorganizational field which constitutes an ecological system. Interaction in this field is analyzed in terms of domain, conflict and coordination, innovation, and responsiveness. This study draws important implications for interorganizational theory and research.

2.1.2 The Rationale for Planning

Dahrendorff, Ralf. ESSAYS IN THE THEORY OF SOCIETY. Stanford, Calif.: Stanford University Press, 1968. x, 300 p.

In "Market and Plan: Two Types of Rationality" (pp. 217-27), Dahrendorff distinguishes between two rational types of social organization. Plan-rational orientation sets purposive social norms but, because it presupposes the possibility of certainty, is unstable and inefficient. Market rationality accepts uncertainty but requires certain plan-rational decisions if it is not to remain an ideology of status-quo participation.

Dyckman, John W. "The Practical Uses of Planning Theory." JOURNAL OF AMERICAN INSTITUTE OF PLANNERS 35 (September 1969): 298-300.

Planning theory is rejected by most planners because of their emphasis on mathematical models, or because it seems to impose formal models of normative decision. But the planner needs a theory of action and decision to defend his intervention. The alternatives are to retreat from the existing basis of professionalism or to modify existing normative models of public action. Examples of such modification are suggested.

Hardin, Garrett. "The Tragedy of the Commons." SCIENCE 162 (13 December 1968): 1243-48.

This seminal article develops the case of individually rational decisions leading to collective irrationality and ruin. This must be avoided by social arrangements involving "mutual coercion mutually agreed on."

Michael, Donald N. THE UNPREPARED SOCIETY: PLANNING FOR A PRECARIOUS FUTURE. New York: Basic Books, 1968. 132 p.

An argument which deduces the need for long-range planning from the increasing acceleration of social change. Michael recognizes the limitations of prediction, however, and suggests a planning process much more adaptive than at present.

Miller, S.M. "Planning: Can It Make a Difference in Capitalist America?" SOCIAL POLICY 6 (September-October 1975): 12-23.

A critique of planning goals and practice from a radical perspective. The author concludes that, in spite of the inherent biases of the system and of the danger that planning will fail to articulate the right social goals, planning is desirable for the gains it promises in increasing the visibility of political and economic processes and results.

Skjei, Stephen S. "Urban Problems and the Theoretical Justification of Urban Planning." URBAN AFFAIRS QUARTERLY 11 (March 1975): 323-44.

A review and critique of planners' claims to legitimacy is followed by a proposal for a normative theory of planning based on information provision as a professional purpose in the context of value diversity and conflict in the planning environment.

Vickers, Geoffrey. FREEDOM IN A ROCKING BOAT: CHANGING VALUES IN AN UNSTABLE SOCIETY. London: Allan Lane, 1970. 215 p.

Three fields are identified where accelerating change threatens survival: the physical, the institutional, and the cultural. An argument is made for specific types of regulation to counter this threat: they include general governmental and sectoral. But the limits of regulation are recognized in the need for consent and consensus, which are often absent.

_____. VALUE SYSTEMS AND SOCIAL PROCESS. New York: Basic Books, 1968. xxii, 216 p.

In his essay "Planning and Policy Making" (pp. 96-111), Vickers defines planning as the assistance which experts give in policy development: in problem definition, analysis, and evaluation of alternative solutions. The potential of the planning-programming-budgeting system (PPBS) is discussed, with special reference to the need to explicate non-quantifiable values.

Wildavsky, Aaron. "Does Planning Work?" THE PUBLIC INTEREST 24 (Summer 1971): 95-104.

In the course of a review of Stephen Cohen's MODERN CAPITALIST PLANNING (see p. 68), Wildavsky defines planning in its relation to implementation and future action. By this definition he examines the planning process, using Cohen's French example as a case and referring to other examples of national planning. His conclusion is that planning fails to meet its objectives, as it implies a degree of control over the future which is impossible to attain in any realistic context.

2.2 PLANNING THEORY

2.2.1 Planning Theory and Models

Allison, Lincoln A. ENVIRONMENTAL PLANNING: A POLITICAL AND PHILOSOPHICAL ANALYSIS. Totowa, N.J.: Rowman and Littlefield, 1975. 134 p.

Allison discusses the nature of planning, looking at it as an ideological activity rather than a technical exercise. The development of planning, its relation to politics, and the theories and assumptions behind environmental policy are examined, with a focus on the role of participation and pressure groups in Britain today.

Alonso, William. "Beyond the Inter-Disciplinary Approach to Planning." JOURNAL OF AMERICAN INSTITUTE OF PLANNERS 37 (May 1971): 169-73.

A critique of the traditional interdisciplinary team approach to planning problems. The author proposes an urban and regional discipline, which would consist of specialists from both the "hard" and the "soft" social sciences with metadisciplinary competences.

Banham, Reyner, et al. "Non-Plan: An Experiment in Freedom." NEW SO-
CIETY 338 (20 March 1969): 435-41.

> A critique of the accepted basis and value judgments of planning
> is expressed in a proposal to institutionalize "non-planning" on an
> experimental basis in three selected areas in Britain. Scenarios are
> developed illustrating the possible results of such an experiment,
> which might afford channels for expressing the spontaneity and vi-
> tality to which contemporary planning only pays lip service.

Bolan, Richard S. "Community Decision Behavior: The Culture of Planning."
JOURNAL OF AMERICAN INSTITUTE OF PLANNERS 35 (September 1969):
301-10.

> The author develops a taxonomy of planning types affected by five
> basic variable sets: the process steps, process roles, the decision
> field, strategies, and issue attributes. These types are then char-
> acterized as tending toward action or inaction. Bolan concludes
> that there is a delicate balance between the substance and process
> of planning, and that the planner's main task is to coordinate and
> motivate others, from whom he cannot divorce his traditional sources
> of authority.

Branch, Melville C. URBAN PLANNING THEORY. Stroudsburg, Pa.: Dowden, Hutchinson, and Ross, 1975. 596 p.

> A compilation of selected readings, covering aspects of urban
> planning and the urban environment. These are categorized into
> "legacy," covering the ideological, historical, and regulatory
> background of planning, "design," "form," "information," "process,"
> "analysis," "simulation," "management," "institution," "environ-
> ment," and "emerging concepts." The political aspects of plan-
> ning and its context are touched on only under "emerging concepts"
> which include Lindblom's 1959 article on "muddling through"--an
> indication of how dated these concepts are. The bulk of these
> readings date from the mid-sixties, as does the idea of planning
> conveyed in this book.

Cartwright, Timothy J. "Problems, Solutions and Strategies: A Contribution
to the Theory and Practice of Planning." JOURNAL OF AMERICAN INSTI-
TUTE OF PLANNERS 39 (May 1973): 179-87.

> This paper suggests that the nature of a problem governs both the
> possible solutions and strategies. Four problem types are identi-
> fied: simple, compound, and complex problems, and metaproblems,
> with their corresponding strategies. The author concludes that there
> is a dilemma in the link between problem definition and choice of
> strategy.

Chadwick, George. A SYSTEMS VIEW OF PLANNING: TOWARDS A THEORY
OF THE URBAN AND REGIONAL PLANNING PROCESS. Oxford: Pergamon
Press, 1971. 390 p.

This ambitious attempt at a general planning theory is based on a synthesis of information theory and systems concepts into traditional planning models. Chadwick's model of planning is basically the rational decision making process, with a bow toward Simon's "satisfycing" and Lindblom's incrementalism. He holds out high hopes of the utilization in planning of simulation and predictive models at various levels of sophistication, but pays only lip service to the political and social context of planning activities.

Christakis, Alexander N. "The Limits of Systems Analysis in Economic and Social Development Planning." EKISTICS 34 (July 1972): 34–42.

Because of the speed of contemporary social and technological change, the author asserts the irrelevance of traditional extrapolative methods of planning. He proposes a model of "futures-creative" planning, which would develop scenarios of alternative futures as a framework for public debate.

Cross, Nigel; Elliott, David; and Ray, Robin, eds. MAN MADE FUTURES: READINGS IN SOCIETY, TECHNOLOGY AND DESIGN. London: Hutchinson & Co., 1974. 365 p.

The three sections of this book deal with "Technology and Society," "Policy and Participation," and "Design and Technology." Includes contributions on "Utopia and Technology" (Leiss), "Technology, Planning and Organization" (Galbraith), "A Rationale for Participation" (Stringer), "Planning and Protest" (Page), "The Design Activity" (Alexander), "Wicked Problems" (Rittell and Webber), and "Alternative Technology" (Clarke).

Davidoff, Paul. "Normative Planning." In PLANNING FOR DIVERSITY AND CHOICE, edited by Stanford Anderson, pp. 173–87. Cambridge: MIT Press, 1968.

A proposal for pluralist planning as opposed to single agency planning, in recognition of the distributional implications of solutions which are usually proposed. The author suggests that central planning agencies recognize that their norms are only one of a possible set of views, and that the planning process should enable consideration of outside groups' alternatives.

Doh, Joon Chien. THE PLANNING-PROGRAMMING-BUDGETING SYSTEM IN THREE FEDERAL AGENCIES. New York: Praeger, 1971. xx, 192 p.

A study of the Department of Agriculture (USDA), HEW, and NASA, to ascertain the progress of this system and its application. The results showed that the effectiveness of PPBS was associated with agency head support, staffing, and perception of the measurability of its output. Application of PPBS appeared to be a function of funding incentives, which were highest for USDA, and lowest for NASA.

Doxiadis, Constantinos A. EKISTICS: AN INTRODUCTION TO THE SCIENCE OF HUMAN SETTLEMENT. New York: Oxford University Press, 1968. xxix, 527 p.

In the first part of this book, Doxiadis explains the need for Ekistics, defines it, and relates it to other sciences. In the second part, he discusses the functions and forms of settlements and traces their development toward the universal city of "Ecumenopolis." The third part presents fifty-four "Ekistic Laws," and in the final part Doxiadis presents his development philosophy and planning prescriptions.

Dror, Yehezkel. DESIGN FOR POLICY SCIENCES. Amsterdam: Elsevier, 1971. 156 p.

A presentation of the "scientific revolution" in policy analysis. The contributions of systematic knowledge, structured rationality, and organized creativity are reviewed, and implications are drawn for changes in current patterns of research and policy development.

Dyckman, John W. "New Normative Styles in Urban Studies." PUBLIC ADMINISTRATION REVIEW 31 (May–June 1971): 327–34.

A review and evaluation of planning models and methods, including urban information models, PPBS, advocacy planning, policy analysis, and scenarios. Dyckman believes that the last deserves more extensive use and that, in general, the choice of strategy will be influenced by the decision environment. Though new political models may be emerging, he concludes, bureaucracy is here to stay.

Fainstein, Susan S., and Fainstein, Norman I. "City Planning and Political Values." URBAN AFFAIRS QUARTERLY 6 (March 1971): 341–62.

Four planning types are identified, which correspond to four types of political theory. Traditional planning is linked to the technocratic values; user-oriented social planning reflects democratic majoritarian values; advocacy planning is explicitly political and reflects socialist theory; and incrementalism is really nonplanning and analagous to the economic market system.

Faludi, Andreas. PLANNING THEORY. Oxford: Pergamon Press, 1973. xii, 399 p.

An ambitious attempt, only partially successful, at presenting an integrative theory of planning. Planning strategies, including routinization, sequential decision making, and mixed scanning, are reviewed and analyzed. The author concludes that a salient role of the planner is in the analysis of risks. His contrast of British with U.S. views of planning, relating them to their respective contexts, is useful.

Frieden, Bernard J., and Morris, Robert, eds. URBAN PLANNING AND SO-
CIAL POLICY. New York: Basic Books, 1968. xvii, 459 p. Paperbound.

Twenty-eight papers covering the relationships between planning,
social welfare, race, and poverty, most of them previous journal
publications. Contributions include "Comprehensive Planning and
Social Responsibility" (Webber), "Emerging Patterns in Community
Planning" (Marris and Rein), "Social and Physical Planning for the
Elimination of Poverty" (Gans), "Planning and Politics: Citizen
Participation in Urban Renewal" (Wilson), "Common Goals and the
Linking of Physical and Social Planning" (Perloff), "Client Analy-
sis and the Planning of Public Programs" (Reiner et al.), "Man-
power and the Community Planner's Mandate" (Rein and Marris).

Friedmann, John. "A Conceptual Model for the Analysis of Planning Behavior."
ADMINISTRATIVE SCIENCE QUARTERLY 12 (September 1967): 225-52.

A model is proposed for relating planning types to situational
characteristics and goals. The planning types include developmental and adaptive planning, allocative planning, and innovative
planning. The roles of these planning types are explored in different contexts, and the author does not hesitate to draw normative
implications.

_____. "The Future of Comprehensive Urban Planning: A Critique." PUBLIC
ADMINISTRATION REVIEW 31 (May-June 1971): 315-26.

The comprehensive planning model is criticized for not accounting
for relativity of perceptions and interests, interdependencies, limits
to knowledge and information, and the imperatives of action. A
more adaptive model of planning is called for.

_____. "Notes on Societal Action." JOURNAL OF AMERICAN INSTITUTE
OF PLANNERS 35 (September 1969): 311-18.

Classical model of planning has led to divorce of planning from
implementation. An "action planning" model is proposed which
will fuse action and planning.

_____. RETRACKING AMERICA: A THEORY OF TRANSACTIVE PLANNING.
Garden City, N.Y.: Anchor Press, 1973. xx, 289 p.

This book offers a comprehensive review of planning theory from Karl
Mannheim to the author's own contributions. After an analysis of
the contemporary and prospective societal contexts of planning,
Friedmann proposes a planning model which consists basically of a
process of mutual learning between planners and clients. Included
is a useful annotated bibliography.

Friedmann, John, and Hudson, Barclay [M.]. "Knowledge and Action: A Guide to
Planning Theory." JOURNAL OF AMERICAN INSTITUTE OF PLANNERS 40

(January 1974): 2-16.

A review and taxonomy of planning theories, focusing on their development over time and classifying them by major philosophical traditions. Under planning theories, the authors include a wide range of fields, from welfare economics, through decision theories and organizational development, to empirical urban and national planning studies. The result is a lack of depth in any of these fields and some failure in overall integration.

Friend, John K., and Jessop, W.N. LOCAL GOVERNMENT AND STRATEGIC CHOICE: AN OPERATIONAL RESEARCH APPROACH TO THE PROCESS OF PUBLIC PLANNING. London: Tavistock Publications, 1969. xxvi, 296 p.

A model of sequential decision making is developed and presented in the context of local development planning in Great Britain. This study offers an unusual combination of normative analytical models with descriptive analysis of realistic planning situations, theoretical and pragmatic at once.

Friend, John K.; Power, J.M.; and Yewlett, C.J.L. PUBLIC PLANNING: THE INTER CORPORATE DIMENSION. London: Tavistock Publications, 1974. xxviii, 533 p.

The field of policy concerns is defined as the "management of local and regional change." The authors' analytical perspective is the theory of strategic change, with which they analyze cases in local and regional planning. Detailed analysis is devoted to a case study. The study concludes with a series of general propositions about planning in complex organizational environments.

Grabow, Stephen, and Heskin, Allan. "Foundations for a Radical Concept of Planning." (With commentary by Amitai Etzioni.) JOURNAL OF AMERICAN INSTITUTE OF PLANNERS 39 (March 1973): 106-14.

Advocates the change of planning goals and its internal structure from its current tendencies of elite-perpetuation and resistance to change. A new paradigm is proposed to challenge the "rational-comprehensive model," which will consist of the facilitation of change by synthesizing rational action with spontaneity in the context of a decentralized communal society.

Kalba, Kas. "Postindustrial Planning: A Review Forward." JOURNAL OF AMERICAN INSTITUTE OF PLANNERS 40 (May 1974): 147-55.

Kalba projects a number of planning issues into the context of Daniel Bell's THE COMING OF POST-INDUSTRIAL SOCIETY (New York: Basic Books, 1976). These include the conflict between technocratic-centralized and participatory planning, the problem of coping with information overload, and the integration of political competition. He concludes that planning methodologies must become more adaptable and strive for maximum robustness.

Klaasen, Leo H., and Paelinck, Jean H.P. INTEGRATION OF SOCIO-ECONOMIC AND PHYSICAL PLANNING: REPORT PREPARED FOR THE UNITED NATIONS CENTRE FOR HOUSING, BUILDING AND PLANNING. Rotterdam: Rotterdam University Press, 1974. 69 p.

This report is based on the recognition that effective planning needs an interdisciplinary approach. It advocates a more comprehensive integration of social, economic, and physical planning.

Krieger, Martin H. "Some New Directions for Planning Theories." JOURNAL OF AMERICAN INSTITUTE OF PLANNERS 40 (May 1974): 156–63.

Three "binds" of existing planning theories are identified: the desire for a formal generalized theory, the alienation of people objectified in such a theory, and the lack of "impersonation" in self-reflective planning theories. Krieger proposes the incorporation of insights from phenomenology, linguistics, and social psychology into planning theory.

Ozbekhan, Hasan. "Toward a General Theory of Planning." In PERSPECTIVES ON PLANNING: PROCEEDINGS OF THE OECD WORKING SYMPOSIUM ON LONG-RANGE FORECASTING AND PLANNING, edited by Erich Jantsch, pp. 47–158. Paris: OECD, 1968.

Objecting to planning in a purely predictive mode, the author attempts to develop an integrative multilevel planning process which distinguishes between three levels of planning: operational, strategic, and normative. This paper of the Organization for Economic and Cooperative Development includes prescriptions for planning at each of these levels, but its usefulness is limited by its abstraction from any realistic social environment.

Rondinelli, Dennis A. URBAN AND REGIONAL DEVELOPMENT PLANNING: POLICY AND ADMINISTRATION. Ithaca, N.Y.: Cornell University Press, 1975. 272 p.

A review of the development of planning theory and analysis of traditional planning models concludes with the proposal of a political- and policy-related planning process. Illustrations are taken from cases in urban and regional development, one of which, in upstate Pennsylvania, is presented in great detail. Though the innovative contribution of this work to planning theory is limited, it is a useful summary of developments to date.

_____. "Urban Planning as Policy Analysis: Management of Urban Change." JOURNAL OF AMERICAN INSTITUTE OF PLANNERS 39 (January 1973): 13–22.

Rondinelli offers planners the role of urban policy analysts. He suggests that new techniques and methods need to be developed for this role, and that planners must receive cognitive inputs and skills to deal with complex policymaking systems. These focus mainly on conflict resolution and political interaction.

Sennett, Richard. THE USES OF DISORDER. New York: Knopf, 1970. xvii, 108 p.

A critique of the traditional comprehensive planning approach, based on its propensity to physical solutions, planners' middle-class norms and their avoidance of urban complexity, leads to an advocacy of a "new anarchism." This is a neighborhood-centered planning model involving voluntary regulation and self-enforcement by local "survival" communities.

2.2.2 Process, Context, and Roles

Allensworth, Don T. THE POLITICAL REALITIES OF URBAN PLANNING. New York: Praeger, 1975. x, 188 p.

A concise synthesis of all the political elements making up the context of the American urban planning process. Covers city politics; suburban politics; the planning commission; the planning bureaucracy; local, metropolitan, and state agencies; federal agencies and the judiciary; interest groups; and political parties. Depth is sacrificed for breadth, but conceptual organization is good; excellent textbook.

Altschuler, Alan. THE CITY PLANNING PROCESS: A POLITICAL ANALYSIS. Ithaca, N.Y.: Cornell University Press, 1965. x, 466 p.

In one of the earliest empirical studies of the planning process, Altschuler presents and analyzes several case studies of planning at the local level to compare formal models of rational planning with the type of planning actually carried out. His conclusions are that planning is a more politicized process than allowed for in prescriptions of the rational model, and that the role of technician may in some contexts be too limiting, though in others it is effective in ensuring survival, at least.

Barr, Donald A. "The Professional Urban Planner." JOURNAL OF AMERICAN INSTITUTE OF PLANNERS 38 (May 1972): 155-59.

Barr attempts to explode the "myths" of the planner as artist and creator and of comprehensive rationality. He concludes that the professional planner today produces, at worst, mediocre plans which are little more than projections of reality. At best, the planner is an agent of government, and planning is a vital bureaucratic function.

Benveniste, Guy. THE POLITICS OF EXPERTISE. Berkeley, Calif.: Glendessary Press, 1972. ix, 232 p.

A detailed description and analysis of education planning in Mexico, focusing on the relations between the technically expert planners, the politicians, and bureaucrats. The planners proved effective in cases where their proposals conveyed an image which could serve as a focus for political mobilization. Benveniste distinguishes between four types of planning: "trivial," which reinforces the status quo; "utopian," basically image-making; "imperative," top-down planning contiguous with an agency's or an official's resources and power; and "intentional," which involves the interplay between different spheres of authority and, depending on the multiplier effect between them, is suitable to complex and uncertain situations.

Bolan, Richard S. "The Social Relations of the Planner." JOURNAL OF AMERICAN INSTITUTE OF PLANNERS 37 (November 1971): 386-96.

Bolan analyzes the planning process in terms of a planning role, a client role, and a community decision network--all interacting around a public agenda. He suggests that traditional models of planning imply simplistic assumptions about the social setting, and that this conceptual framework will give the planner greater awareness of situational variables.

Bolan, Richard S., and Nuttall, Ronald L. URBAN PLANNING AND POLITICS. Lexington, Mass.: D.C. Heath, 1975. xviii, 211 p.

The book opens with a discussion of the dilemmas of planning and politics; next, a summary of the findings is presented, followed by a review of previous literature and a presentation of Bolan's model of community decision making. Four case studies are described: the Boston Inner Belt, the Manhattan Expressway, the Pittsburgh Great High Schools Plan, and the Boston Affiliated Hospitals Center. They are analysed applying a "qualitative test" to two-variables in the model, "actor attributes" and "decision field attributes," while other variables were "held constant." In the light of the findings, the authors suggest some modifications of their model and offer some new perspectives for a theory of planned social change.

Boskoff, Alvin. THE SOCIOLOGY OF URBAN REGIONS. New York: Appleton-Century-Crofts, 1962. xvi, 389 p.

One of the most interesting attempts to develop a sociology of cities and place the planning process within that framework. While this book received much criticism in the journals, we believe it is a major contribution.

Erber, Ernest, ed. URBAN PLANNING IN TRANSITION. New York: Grossman, 1970. xxviii, 323 p.

A compilation of American Institute of Planners sponsored papers, in three parts: "The Societal Framework," "The State of the Art," and "The Professional Planner's Role." Contributions include "Toward a National Policy for Planning the Environment" (Eldredge),

"Social Planning in the American Democracy" (Dyckman), "The Rational Use of Urban Space as Public Policy" (Blumenfeld), "The Emergence of the States in Urban Affairs" (Kaunitz), "Identifying the Public Interest: Values and Goals" (Wheaton), "The Changing Role of the Planner in the Decision Making Process" (Cohen), "Preparing the Profession for its Changing Role" (Wetmore), "The Fuzzy Future of Planning Education" (Mann), and "New Roles in Social Planning" (Frieden).

Eversley, David. THE PLANNER IN SOCIETY: THE CHANGING ROLE OF A PROFESSION. London: Faber and Faber, 1973. 360 p.

Part 3: "The Planner and the Planned"--planning in its societal and community context; part 4: "Towards New Styles of Planning" --concludes with ideologies and values of planning.

Ewing, David W. THE HUMAN SIDE OF PLANNING: TOOL OR TYRANT. New York: Macmillan, 1969. 216 p.

A review of generalized planning activities, addressed to a lay audience. The author believes that some of the defects in rigor of the planning process are among its greatest virtues, as over-rigid planning creates "anti-planning." For effective planning, he emphasizes the need for political involvement and power.

Gans, Herbert J. PEOPLE AND PLANS: ESSAYS ON URBAN PROBLEMS AND SOLUTIONS. New York: Basic Books, 1968. 395 p.

A critique of traditional city planning is offered in these essays. Gans maintains that planners are not user-oriented, that they lack understanding of cities' political and socioeconomic environments, and that their plans have little impact. Areas covered include "Environment and Behavior," "City Planning and Goal-Oriented Planning," "Planning for Suburbs and New Towns," "Planning Against Urban Poverty and Segregation," and "The Racial Crisis."

Heywood, Philip. PLANNING AND HUMAN NEED. Newton Abbot, Eng.: David and Charles, 1974. 192 p.

Heywood analyzes the societal context of planned intervention, raising the question of whose values and objectives should be realized by the planning process. His descriptions are illustrated by cases of planning in housing, urban renewal, and transportation, and he recommends correctives in planning approaches to remedy present defects.

Kahn, Alfred J. THEORY AND PRACTICE OF SOCIAL PLANNING. New York: Russell Sage Foundation, 1969. 348 p.

An analysis of the planning process from the rational decision-making perspective. Kahn focuses on the application of rational decision methods to the design and evaluation of social programs and community planning.

Lichfield, Nathaniel; Kettle, Peter; and Whitbread, Michael. EVALUATION IN THE PLANNING PROCESS. Oxford and New York: Pergamon Press, 1975. 326 p.

The role of evaluation in making decisions in urban and regional planning is the focus of this book. In the first three chapters, a model of the planning process is presented; subsequently, principles and methods of evaluation are discussed with a rich selection of illustrative cases. The approach is pragmatic rather than theoretical, though with no sacrifice of rigor, and this book is a valuable text for practitioners and students alike.

McLoughlin, J. Brian. CONTROL AND URBAN PLANNING. London: Faber and Faber, 1973. 287 p.

A discussion of the statutory framework controlling planning in Great Britain, illustrated by seventeen cases of pre-1974 local planning authorities. The development of positive local and county planning and the evolution of local planning policy is reviewed, using systems concepts as an analytic approach. The author focuses on the data and information needs of the local planning system and projects future patterns of planning and control.

Myerson, Martin, and Banfield, Edward C. POLITICS, PLANNING, AND THE PUBLIC INTEREST. New York: Free Press, 1955. 353 p. Paperbound.

A now-classic study of the interaction of planning and politics in public decision making in the context of the Chicago Public Housing Authority. One of the first works to point out the limitations of the rational planning approach in any realistic context. Banfield's supplement puts the preceding descriptive study into an economic theoretical model. Though over twenty years old, this study is still not dated.

Needleman. GUERRILLAS IN THE BUREAUCRACY. See 2.3.4. (p. 55)

Rabinovitz, Francine F. CITY POLITICS AND PLANNING. New York: Atherton Press, 1969. 192 p.

Based on a survey of six New Jersey cities, the author concludes that neither the planner's organizational position nor the city's political system alone explains variations in effectiveness. But a model relating the two identifies different roles for planners which work in different contexts. Roles include technician, broker, and mobilizer, and Rabinovitz suggests altering professional norms to incorporate this diversity.

Solesbury, William. POLICY IN URBAN PLANNING: STRUCTURE PLANS,

PROGRAMMES AND LOCAL PLANS. Oxford: Pergamon Press, 1974. 186 p.

> This book aims to combine the technical, political, and adminis-
> trative aspects of urban planning in Great Britain. Solesbury
> describes the various plan forms current today and analyzes the
> process of plan making, to develop a rationale for the greater
> integration of process and plan.

2.2.3 Public Values and Planning for Change

Anderson, Stanford, ed. PLANNING FOR DIVERSITY AND CHOICE: POS-
SIBLE FUTURES AND THEIR RELATIONS TO THE MAN-CONTROLLED ENVI-
RONMENT. Cambridge: MIT Press, 1968. 340 p.

> Papers followed by discussion and comment; contributions include
> "Long-range Studies of the Future and their Role in French Plan-
> ning" (Cazes), "The Parameters of Urban Planning" (Duhl), "Ob-
> solescence and 'Obsolescibles' in Planning for the Future" (Maz-
> lish), "Normative Planning" (Davidoff), and "Models as Modes of
> Action" (Feyerabend).

Arrow, Kenneth J. SOCIAL CHOICE AND INDIVIDUAL VALUES. Cowles
Foundation Monograph 12. New York: Wiley, 1963. 124 p.

> A seminal work on the social aggregation of values, dwelling on
> the distinction between social and individual decision processes.
> Based on a set of persuasive axioms, Arrow demonstrates the im-
> possibility of a simple determinate aggregation of individual choices
> into social decisions.

Brooks, Michael P. SOCIAL PLANNING AND CITY PLANNING. Planning
Advisory Service Information Report No. 261. Chicago: American Society
of Planning Officials, September 1970. 61 p. Paperbound.

> The concept of social planning is discussed and the history of its
> development reviewed. Planning is related to social problems, ur-
> ban advocacy, and salient issues of the near future. Includes
> bibliography.

Cowan, Peter, ed. THE FUTURE OF PLANNING. London: Heinemann Educational Books, 1973. 182 p.

> A general review of planning and its prospects, with a British per-
> spective. Contents: "The Tasks for Planning" (Wilmott), "How
> Planning Can Respond to New Issues" (Wilson), "Manpower and
> Education" (Hall), "The Future of the Planning Profession" (Mc-
> Loughlin), "Planning and Government" (Donnison), "Planning and
> the Public" (Senior), "Planning and the Market" (Foster), and
> "Conclusions" (Jones).

Dror, Yehezkel. PUBLIC POLICYMAKING REEXAMINED. San Francisco:

Chandler, 1968. 370 p.

>   The author reviews a series of models of public decision making
>   ranging from the traditional rational model, through incrementalism
>   and "satisfycing," to radical change and metarational models. This
>   analysis is more useful than Dror's conclusion, which proposes a
>   normative "optimal" model which is basically a multistage exten-
>   sion of the rational analytic approach.

Duhl, Leonard. "Planning and Predicting." DAEDALUS, Summer 1967, pp. 779-
88.

>   The planner is seen as an agent of change, with a need to guide
>   change like a therapist. Crisis is the result of misplanning and
>   of the noninvolvement of client groups in the planning process.
>   The planner, therefore, must be sensitive to changes, and planning
>   agencies must be self-renewing organizations which participate with
>   their consumers in the definition of problems.

Dyckman, John W. "Societal Goals and Planned Societies." JOURNAL OF
AMERICAN INSTITUTE OF PLANNERS 32 (March 1966): 66-76.

>   An examination of the role of social planning and planners in the
>   articulation of societal goals. Dyckman asserts the primacy of
>   ideology and of political decision makers in setting public goals,
>   but gives social planning the role of analyzing needs and objec-
>   tives to enable open public debate and public acceptance.

Gross, Bertrand [M.]. "Planning in an Era of Social Revolution." PUBLIC
ADMINISTRATION REVIEW 31 (May-June 1971): 259-96.

>   The contemporary scene is characterized as increasingly changeful,
>   discontinuous, and complex. Attempts at increasing rationality are
>   criticized; rather, a theory of planning is proposed based on social
>   learning.

Haefele, Edwin T. REPRESENTATIVE GOVERNMENT AND ENVIRONMENTAL
MANAGEMENT. Baltimore, Md.: Johns Hopkins Press, 1973. 188 p.

>   Environmental issues are addressed as problems of social change,
>   involving societal decision mechanisms as analyzed by Arrow (see
>   above, this section). The cases of the San Francisco Conservation and
>   Development Commission, the Potomac Basin Commission, and the
>   Twin Cities Metro Council are presented, and the author concludes
>   that considerable institutional redesign is necessary. As conceptual
>   models for such changes he analyzes the Delaware Estuary model,
>   the Dorfman-Jacoby management model, and the Olsen utility
>   model.

Michael, Donald N. LEARNING TO PLAN AND PLANNING TO LEARN:
THE SOCIAL PSYCHOLOGY OF CHANGING TOWARD FUTURE-RESPONSIVE

Theory and Context of Planning

SOCIETAL LEARNING. San Francisco: Jossey-Bass, 1973. 341 p.

The author advocates a new planning model based on the inability of traditional problem solving to address radical processes of social change. This model involves long-range social planning focusing on conjectural prediction and goal-setting, and its implementation will need basic social and organizational changes. Resistances to these changes are identified, but the process of overcoming these resistances is poorly developed.

Moffitt, Leonard C. "Value Implications for Public Planning: Some Thoughts and Questions." JOURNAL OF AMERICAN INSTITUTE OF PLANNERS 41 (November 1975): 397-405.

This article raises questions about value definition and measurement and suggests some innovative techniques. It then addresses the issue of value ownership and proposes a reexamination of traditional assumptions.

Ozbekhan, Hasan. "The Triumph of Technology: 'Can' Implies 'Ought.'" In PLANNING FOR DIVERSITY AND CHOICE, edited by Stanford Anderson, pp. 204-18. Cambridge: MIT Press, 1968.

Ozbekhan criticized the type of planning which is limited to technical-economic alternatives and results in predicting a future based on current feasibility. In feasibility he sees the elevation of a strategic concept to a normative concept. The author makes a plea for the reinstatement of explicitly normative planning.

Vickers, Geoffrey. "Values, Norms and Policies." POLICY SCIENCES 4 (March 1973): 103-12.

Proceeding from definitions of norms and values, Vickers draws the policy implications that goals are determined by the type of control exercised. He identifies five types of control, ranging from control by releaser--basically, a conditioned response--through control by rule, by purpose, or by "norm," to control by self-determination--an ethical debate about values.

Webber, Melvin M. "Planning in an Environment of Change." In PROBLEMS OF AN URBAN SOCIETY. Vol. 3: PLANNING FOR CHANGE, edited by J.B. Cullingworth, pp. 23-66. Toronto: University of Toronto Press, 1973. 195 p.

Webber projects a postindustrial future consisting of rapid change. The implications are radical changes in accepted assumptions of continuity, consensus on and predictability of goals. From its traditions based in technical-social reform, planning needs to redirect itself toward fewer constraints on choice, guiding decisions by outputs of public actions rather than the present habit of imposing input bundles on the basis of planner predetermined images of goodness.

Wheaton, William L.C., and Wheaton, Margaret. "Identifying the Public Interest: Values and Goals." In URBAN PLANNING IN TRANSITION, edited by Ernest Erber, pp. 152–64. New York: Grossman, 1970.

> The Wheatons urge a recognition by planners of the competing goals of individuals and interests. Market aggregation of values is typical in U.S. society. Planners share class biases but have an institutional concern with welfare goals. The importance of bargaining in the political process and of public participation in decision making is illustrated by three cases. The planner's problem is to make choices relevant and meaningful and to devise useful procedures for public consultation.

2.3 THE GOVERNMENTAL CONTEXT

2.3.1 The Federal Government

Aaron, Henry J. SHELTER AND SUBSIDIES: WHO BENEFITS FROM FEDERAL HOUSING POLICIES? Washington, D.C.: Brookings Institution, 1972. 238 p.

> This study criticizes the uncoordinated nature of federal housing policies, by identifying the beneficiaries of some of the largest programs. These include tax subsidies, mortgage guarantees, low-rent public housing, and housing assistance programs. The author concludes that the main benefits go to middle class homeowners, and that subsidies for those in the over $50,000 per annum income class came close to those given in rental assistance to the low-income families. As a solution to these inequities, he proposes a uniform housing assistance plan.

Andrews, Richard N.L. "Three Fronts of Federal Environmental Policy." JOURNAL OF AMERICAN INSTITUTE OF PLANNERS 37 (July 1971): 258–66.

> The three fronts are identified as residuals management and pollution control, environmental quality evaluation and control, and environmental resources planning and management. Needs are identified for better policy; these include operational criteria, better incentives, and increased citizen access.

Barbrook, Alec T. "The Making of a Department." URBAN AFFAIRS QUARTERLY 6 (March 1971): 277–96.

> Traces the background and history of the creation of the Department of Housing and Urban Development, and analyzes its impact in the urban arena.

Beckman, Norman, et al. "Legislative Reviews: Planning and Urban Development 1968-69." JOURNAL OF AMERICAN INSTITUTE OF PLANNERS 36 (September 1970): 345-59; "Development of National Urban Growth Policy:

1972 Congressional and Executive Action." JOURNAL OF AMERICAN INSTI-
TUTE OF PLANNERS 39 (July 1973): 229-43; "National Urban Growth Policy:
1973 Congressional and Executive Action." JOURNAL OF AMERICAN INSTI-
TUTE OF PLANNERS 40 (July 1974): 226-42; "National Urban Growth Policy:
1974 Congressional and Executive Action." JOURNAL OF AMERICAN INSTI-
TUTE OF PLANNERS 41 (July 1975): 234-48.

> A review of federal legislation in the area of planning, urban
> development, and national growth and land management policy,
> appearing annually (with occasional interruptions). This review
> is an excellent single reference for sources of federal programs
> and action over this wide-ranging area.

Bolan, Richard S. "Planning and the New Federalism." JOURNAL OF
AMERICAN INSTITUTE OF PLANNERS 39 (July 1973): 226-28.

> A review of the dimensions of the "New Federalism" which are
> relevant to planning. The new role of government may be a symp-
> tom of the failure of the bureaucratic welfare state, but there is
> the danger of the erosion of the rights of minority interests.

Capoccia, Victor A. "Social Welfare Planning and the New Federalism: The
Allied Services Act." JOURNAL OF AMERICAN INSTITUTE OF PLANNERS 39
(July 1973): 244-53.

> Capoccia analyzes the act and concludes that its potential is
> greater for improving services delivery in a narrow sense than for
> creating a systemwide basis for social welfare service planning.

Clapp, James A. NEW TOWNS AND URBAN POLICY. New York: Dunel-
len, 1971. 342 p.

> A review of new town development in the United States and abroad
> as an instrument of national policy. The case is presented for new
> towns, and the relevance and feasibility of the new towns concept
> for U.S. urban policy is evaluated. Useful for its detailed review
> of federal programs and current U.S. new towns efforts. An ex-
> haustive bibliography is also included.

Derthick, Martha. NEW TOWNS IN TOWN: WHY A FEDERAL PROGRAM
FAILED. Washington, D.C.: Urban Institute, 1972. 103 p. Paperbound.

> Derthick traces the development of the New Towns-In-Town program
> and its implementation during the Johnson administration. The pro-
> gress of six projects is analyzed in detail to discover the reasons
> for the failure of this program. From her conclusions the author
> draws some insightful generalizations on the limits of centrally con-
> ceived and planned federal programs when they have to be exe-
> cuted at the local level.

Donovan, John C. THE POLITICS OF POVERTY. 2d ed. Indianapolis:
Bobbs-Merrill, 1973. 201 p.

The genesis and implementation at the federal level of the Office of Economic Opportunity and the Johnson administration's poverty programs. While these programs were grand in concept, it is pointed out that they failed largely due to a lack of commitment in implementation. Maximum feasible participation is also discussed, and it is mentioned that not only legislators did not recognize its implications, but that it was also misinterpreted by almost all program designers.

Frieden, Bernard J., and Kaplan, Marshall. THE POLITICS OF NEGLECT: URBAN AID FROM MODEL CITIES TO REVENUE SHARING. Cambridge: MIT Press, 1975. 281 p.

Frieden and Kaplan, both deeply involved in the implementation of federal urban programs, review the Model Cities program from its origin to its implementation, and evaluate two subsequent federal efforts, general and special revenue sharing. They draw conclusions from Model Cities' failures and the shortfall between aspirations and realization, which can be applied to the future design of programs for urban aid.

Ginzburg, Eli, and Solow, Robert M., eds. "The Great Society: Lessons for the Future." THE PUBLIC INTEREST 34 (Special Issue: Winter 1974). 220 p.

Includes: "Social Intervention in a Democracy" (Liebman), "Reform Follows Reality: The Growth of Welfare" (Steiner), "What Does It Do for the Poor? A New Test for National Policy" (Lampman), "The Successes and Failures of Federal Housing Policy" (Downs), and "Some Lessons of the 1960's" (Ginzberg and Solow).

Golany, Gideon, ed. STRATEGIES FOR NEW COMMUNITY DEVELOPMENT IN THE UNITED STATES. Stroudsburg, Pa.: Dowden, Hutchinson, and Ross, 1975. 293 p.

Eleven essays covering problems of new community development ranging from theoretical to pragmatic. The book includes contributions from HUD officials analyzing new communities development from the federal perspective, essays on state policy in Pennsylvania (Hand), the role of the private developer (Simon), an evaluation of the successes and failures of Columbia, Maryland (Weakland), and the economic planning process (Leisch).

Haar, Charles M. BETWEEN THE IDEA AND THE REALITY: A STUDY OF ORIGIN, FATE, AND LEGACY OF THE MODEL CITIES PROGRAM. Boston: Little, Brown, 1975. 359 p.

A personal document from one of the major participants in the development of the program, tracing its ideological influences and legislative, history in great detail. The program's contributions and failures are analyzed, with a view to developing the implications for future program design and implementation. The author concludes by recommending a return to the national urban goals approach and offers a list of possible federal objectives.

Kaplan, Marshall. "Federal Existentialism, Planning, and Social Change: The Oakland, California Task Force." In PROCEEDINGS OF THE AMERICAN INSTITUTE OF PLANNERS FIFTH BIENNIAL GOVERNMENT RELATIONS AND PLANNING POLICY CONFERENCE, pp. 21-29. Washington, D.C.: American Institute of Planners, 1969.

> The origin and structure of the Oakland Task Force as a coordinative and evaluative agency are described, and its findings are presented. These focus on the degree or lack of coordination in the federal decision-making process and its impact on the local delivery of programs and services. The author concludes that a re-examination of the planner's role is needed.

LeGates, Richard T., and Morgan, Mary C. "The Perils of Special Revenue Sharing for Community Development." JOURNAL OF AMERICAN INSTITUTE OF PLANNERS 39 (July 1973): 254-64.

> Special revenue sharing is projected to bring less funding to cities, increased roles for local and state governments, and fewer incentives to attack inequities. Amendments are proposed to correct these defects, but in principle the return of community development to the unfettered control of local governments is opposed.

Levine, Robert A. PUBLIC PLANNING: FAILURE AND REDIRECTION. New York: Basic Books, 1972. 206 p.

> With a focus on planning at the federal level, this book relates planning failures to the kinds of systems that are designed. The author distinguishes between highly administered systems, at one extreme, and decentralized, self-administering market-like systems, at the other. The book's argument is presented through numerous cases, ranging from New Deal programs, as examples of comprehensively planned systems, to federal tax incentives, as a case of a decentralized market-oriented program. In relating planning to implementation, the author also comes to grips with the organizational characteristics of bureaucracy and their effect on the results of planning efforts. This book's conclusions and prescriptions are of profound importance to planners and policy makers alike.

Levitan, Sar A., and Zickler, K. THE QUEST FOR A FEDERAL MANPOWER PARTNERSHIP. Cambridge, Mass.: Harvard University Press, 1975. 131 p.

> A short essay on the federal manpower legislation which culminated in the Comprehensive Employment and Training Act of 1973. Its utilization and effectiveness is analyzed in six case studies: Albuquerque, Boston, Cleveland, Milwaukee, San Diego, and Washington, D.C.

Pressman, Jeffrey L., and Wildavsky, Aaron. IMPLEMENTATION. Berkeley and Los Angeles: University of California Press, 1973. 200 p.

A case study of the development and implementation of the Economic Development Administration program in Oakland, California. Important inferences are drawn about the complexities of joint action between multiple governmental participants and the fallacy of social experimentation. The authors conclude that policy development must be closely related to the difficulties of implementation. A useful appendix exposes the paucity of literature on implementation.

Rondinelli, Dennis A. "Politics of Law Making and Implementation: The Case of Regional Policy." JOURNAL OF URBAN LAW 59 (February 1973): 403–47.

The emergence of regional development legislation is described, and its failures in application are analyzed. Reasons for failure include hybrid planning agencies, rational planning in a pluralistic environment, conflicting problems and interests, amorphous goals, and methodological difficulties. The proponents of regional development assistance learned that politics are inextricably involved in both legislation and implementation.

_____. "Revenue Sharing and American Cities: Analysis of the Federal Experiment in Local Assistance." JOURNAL OF AMERICAN INSTITUTE OF PLANNERS 41 (September 1975): 319–33.

This analysis of the impacts of revenue sharing concludes that few of its broad objectives have been attained. Recommendations are proposed for a three-pronged system of federal aid which will be more effective in creating a "New Federalism."

Rothblatt, Donald N. "National Development Policy." PUBLIC ADMINISTRATION REVIEW 34 (July–August 1974): 369–76.

The author proposes institutionalizing a national development policy, which has become timely because of migration, socioeconomic, and environmental problems. He suggests a number of possible goals and a strategy consisting of encouraging urban development in rural areas and mid-sized communities. A new federal entity is suggested to coordinate this effort.

Sax, Joseph L. DEFENDING THE ENVIRONMENT: A STRATEGY FOR CITIZEN ACTION. New York: Knopf, 1971. 252 p.

A series of case studies is presented to illustrate citizen involvement in environmental issues. These cover both administrative procedures and legal approaches. An appendix offers a model environmental law which has been adopted by the Michigan legislature.

Schick, Allen. "A Death in the Bureaucracy: The Demise of Federal PPBS." PUBLIC ADMINISTRATION REVIEW 33 (March-April 1973): 146-56.

> An evaluation of the successes and failures of PPBS at the federal level on the occasion of its official discontinuance. It failed to be the change agent envisaged but left a legacy of improved analytic capability. Its failure was due to its conflict-enhancing character, in contrast to the conflict-abatement mechanisms of traditional budgeting.

Schultze, Charles L. THE POLITICS AND ECONOMICS OF PUBLIC SPEND-ING. Washington, D.C.: Brookings Institution, 1969. 143 p.

> An analysis of the governmental planning and decision-making process by a long-time insider, well illustrated with cases. Schultze makes the case for the possibility and desirability of rationalizing government allocation decisions. PPBS is suggested as a possible tool but qualified by a realistic awareness of its limitations.

Solomon, Arthur. HOUSING THE URBAN POOR: A CRITICAL EVALUATION OF FEDERAL HOUSING POLICY. Cambridge: MIT Press, 1974. 227 p.

> A systematic analysis of the housing policy choices facing U.S. decision makers. Applying realistic constraints, the author develops five options: eliminating all federal support, retaining tax and mortgage insurance provisions only, new low-income housing construction, consumer subsidy, and a combination of the latter two. Solomon's evaluation of the impacts of these policies concludes that new construction has been overemphasized as a redistributive tool, and leased public housing in existing units is found to be the most cost-effective policy.

Williams, Walter. SOCIAL POLICY RESEARCH AND ANALYSIS: THE EXPERI-ENCE IN THE FEDERAL SOCIAL AGENCIES. New York: Elsevier, 1971. 204 p.

> Williams's personal experience provides the foundations for this study of the utilization of social science research techniques in the planning and evaluation of social programs at the federal level. Detailed suggestions are offered to improve the development and use of policy-relevant research, stressing the types of research which will be most useful for decision making and the changes needed in the bureaucratic environment to stimulate evaluative analysis and utilization.

Wolman, Harold. THE POLITICS OF FEDERAL HOUSING. New York: Dodd, Mead, 1971. 227 p.

> Wolman describes and analyzes the dynamics of the federal housing policy process, based on data and interviews collected during the Johnson administration. He examines the political and organiza-

tional environment and identifies four major components of the
conversion process which creates policy outputs from environmental
demands: they are policy formulation, legislation, appropriations,
and operationalization.

2.3.2 State Planning

American Assembly, Columbia University. THE STATES AND THE URBAN CRI-
SIS. Englewood Cliffs, N.J.: Prentice-Hall, 1970. 215 p.

> Scholars, journalists, and practitioners examine the states' response
> to metropolitinization trends and the urban crisis. Urban problems
> are identified, and the obstacles to state action are analyzed.
> These are divided into constitutional, fiscal, and political cate-
> gories. A contribution by John N. Kolesar focuses on state
> planning, state development corporations, and state involvement in
> federal programs.

Bickner, Robert E. "Science at the Service of Government: California Tries
to Exploit an Unnatural Resource." POLICY SCIENCES 3 (July 1972): 183-
99.

> Bickner reviews the experience of the State of California in enlist-
> ing aerospace firms, the State Assembly Science & Technology Ad-
> visory Council, and "think tanks" like the Rand Institute, to ad-
> dress policy problems. He concludes that the difficulties in ap-
> plying "scientific" analysis to policy issues lie less with their
> limited use than with reluctance to admit the limitations of rig-
> orous conventional analytic methods.

Council of State Governments. Task Force on Natural Resources and Land Use
Information and Technology. ORGANIZATION, MANAGEMENT, AND FI-
NANCING OF STATE LAND USE PROGRAMS. Its Land Use Policy and Pro-
gram Analysis, no. 3. Lexington, Ky.: 1974. 84 p. Paperbound.

> A report of the task force based on a survey of practices in
> Arizona, Arkansas, Colorado, Florida, Maine, Minnesota, Nebras-
> ka, Oregon, and Vermont. Findings are discussed in the context
> of the proposed National Land Use Policy and Planning Assistance
> Act (S.268). The demise of this bill limits their usefulness, but
> if it is revived in some form these findings will be relevant again.

Goldschmidt, Leopold [A.]. PRINCIPLES AND PROBLEMS OF STATE PLANNING.
Planning Advisory Information Service Report No. 247. Chicago: American
Society of Planning Officials, June 1969. 16 p. Paperbound.

> The author develops a set of principles for state planning which
> aim to guide planners beyond the current practice of attempting
> to encompass all aspects of state development within one single
> rational framework.

Harkell, Elizabeth. "New Directions in State Environmental Planning."
JOURNAL OF AMERICAN INSTITUTE OF PLANNERS 37 (July 1971): 253-58.

The following trends in state environmental planning are identified
and analyzed: organizational consolidation, statewide land use
control programs, and regional waste management planning with
state assistance. The author concludes that the midlevel state
perspective is well suited to environmental planning and management.

Krueckeberg, Donald A. "State Environmental Planning: Requirements Vs.
Behavior." JOURNAL OF AMERICAN INSTITUTE OF PLANNERS 38 (November 1972): 392-96.

This paper analyzes data on state planning and effectiveness to
estimate the effect of increased requirements on performance and
to explore the linkages between various planning sectors. Krueicke-
berg finds that requirements are only weakly related to performance
and that mutual reinforcement of various planning activities does
not take place. The implication is that changing the behavior of
state agencies is a complex problem which requires greater understanding than we have.

Moore, Vincent J. "Politics, Planning, and Power in New York State: The
Path from Theory to Reality." JOURNAL OF AMERICAN INSTITUTE OF PLAN-
NERS 37 (March 1971): 66-77.

An analysis of planning and implementation in New York State
through the Rockefeller administration. These consisted of a detailed state land use and settlement policy, and four implementation strategies: regionalization, PPBS, governmental reorganization,
and the use of public benefit corporations.

Rosebaugh, David L. "State Planning as a Policy-Coordinative Process."
JOURNAL OF AMERICAN INSTITUTE OF PLANNERS 42 (January 1976): 52-
63.

This paper analyzes five approaches in state planning for their relative success, service, development, policy, and coordination.
These are combinations of the following orientations: development,
policy, and coordinative. The study concludes that the policy-
coordinative approach is the most effective.

Slavin, Richard H., and Patton, H. Milton, eds. STATE PLANNING ISSUES.
Lexington, Ky.: Council of State Governments and Council of State Planning
Agencies, May 1973. 43 p. Paperbound.

Includes contributions on land use and environmental quality,
Maine's experience in state land use policy, state planning evaluation, state planning and the governor's office, and the death of
the environmental movement (the last perhaps a bit premature).

Spicer, Richard B. INCREASING STATE AND REGIONAL POWER IN THE DEVELOPMENT PROCESS. Planning Advisory Information Service Report No. 255. Chicago: American Society of Planning Officials, March 1970. 35 p. Paperbound.

> This report examines recent state legislation in seven states which reflect a trend toward greater state involvement in local planning and development. These laws enable the state or specified region to regulate land use, review, and where necessary override local ordinances.

2.3.3 Regional Planning

Alden, Jeremy, and Morgan, Robert. REGIONAL PLANNING: A COMPRE-HENSIVE VIEW. New York: Wiley, 1974. 364 p.

> This book aims to synthesize the current state of regional planning and suggests areas for future improvement. Each chapter covers a different aspect (housing, transportation, etc.) and offers examples from European and American ideas and practice.

Berry, David, and Steiker, Gene. "The Concept of Justice in Regional Planning: Justice as Fairness." JOURNAL OF AMERICAN INSTITUTE OF PLANNERS 40 (November 1974): 414-21.

> A strategy for formulating decisions according to their distributional aspects is presented, involving three major elements: the interested parties, their claims, and decision makers' objectivity, with a focus on the question of measurability. The authors conclude that losses are more important than a summary of net gains over losses.

Cooper. "Regional Planning and Implementation." See 2.5.2 (p. 69)

Derthick, Martha. BETWEEN STATE AND NATION: REGIONAL ORGANIZATIONS OF THE U.S. Washington, D.C.: Brookings Institution, 1974. 242 p.

> This work surveys the history, performance, and impacts of regional agencies in the United States. Cases include the Tennessee Valley Authority, the Delaware River Basin Commission, the Appalachian Regional Commission, the Title II River Basin Planning Commissions, and the Federal Regional Councils. The author concludes that the specific type of regional organization adopted should depend on local circumstances, but that the most generalizable form is that of the Appalachian Regional Commission.

Dunham, David M., and Hilhorst, Jos. G.M., eds. ISSUES IN REGIONAL PLANNING. The Hague: Institute of Social Sciences, 1971. 275 p.

> Papers from a 1970 conference addressing (1) "Education for Regional Planning," (2) "Regional Planning and Development"--theory

and cases, (3) "Recognition of Regional Planning," (4) "Public Participation in Regional Planning," and (5) "Administration of Regional Development."

Friedmann, John. REGIONAL DEVELOPMENT POLICY: A CASE STUDY OF VENEZUELA. Cambridge: MIT Press, 1966. 279 p.

The author's model of core-periphery regional development is presented in the context of the development of the Guyana region of Venezuela. Focuses on the relation between spatial patterns and system-wide growth, in an attempt to develop an explanatory theory of regional development.

Friedmann, John, and Alonso, William, eds. REGIONAL POLICY: READINGS IN THEORY AND APPLICATIONS. Cambridge: MIT Press, 1975. 808 p.

An update of the same editors' 1964 reader, including the following: "Location Theory" (Alonso), "The Nature of Economic Regions" (Loesch), "Regional Inequality and the Process of National Development" (Williamson), "Internal and External Factors in the Development of Urban Economies" (Thompson), "Spatial Organization of Power in the Development of Urban Systems" (Friedmann), "Growth in Subnational Regions" (Perloff, North, Tiebout, and Nichols), "The Cultural Role of Cities" (Redfield and Singer), "The City in Informational Society" (Sanuki), "The Economics of Urban Size" (Alonso), "The Urban Poor" (Nelson), "Growth Poles--a Review" (Darwent), "Criteria for a Growth Center Policy" (Hansen), and "Urban and Regional Imbalances for a National Strategy of Urbanization" (Alonso). The final chapter presents a useful series of case studies in regional planning, including France, Israel, Spain, Turkey, and the United States, and an excellent bibliographical essay (Friedmann) covering the last decade of regional development planning literature.

Gertler. PLANNING THE CANADIAN ENVIRONMENT. See 2.5.2. (p. 70)

_____. REGIONAL PLANNING IN CANADA. See 2.5.2. (p. 70)

Hoffmann. REGIONAL DEVELOPMENT STRATEGIES IN SOUTHEAST EUROPE. See 2.5.1 (p. 67)

Levin, Melvin R. COMMUNITY AND REGIONAL PLANNING: ISSUES IN PUBLIC POLICY. Praeger Special Studies in U.S. Economic, Social, and Political Issues. 3d ed. New York: Praeger, 1977. 340 p.

A collection of Levin's essays on topics including metropolitan planning, transportation, area development, state planning, social indicators, and PPBS.

Manners. REGIONAL DEVELOPMENT IN GREAT BRITAIN. See 2.5.3 (p. 73)

Mogulof, Melvin B. "The Federal Regional Councils: A Potential Instrument for Planning and Joint Action." SOCIAL SCIENCE REVIEW 2 (June 1970): 132-46.

> The development of regional councils is described, and their goals, structure, and intergovernmental relations reviewed. The author concedes that they have no authority, but identifies their main functions as identifying points of conflict and improving problem solving through monitoring and coordination.

_____. "Regional Planning, Clearance and Evaluation: A Look at the A-95 Process." JOURNAL OF AMERICAN INSTITUTE OF PLANNERS 37 (November 1971): 418-22.

> The operation of the A-95 federal grant review process in the context of regional planning is examined. Its failure, the author concludes, lies in its inability to discriminate between proposals from a regional point of view. He suggests that this process be used as a vehicle to encourage regional plan development to enable adequate evaluation.

Rodwin. PLANNING URBAN GROWTH AND REGIONAL DEVELOPMENT. See 2.5.3 (p. 74)

Rondinelli. "Politics of Law Making and Implementation." See 2.3.1 (p. 45)

Rothblatt, Donald N. "Rational Planning Reexamined." JOURNAL OF AMERICAN INSTITUTE OF PLANNERS 37 (January 1971): 26-37.

> The Appalachian regional planning program is studied to evaluate the feasibility of the rational planning model. While this model is found to be substantially applicable, it was limited by the unwillingness of decision makers to operationalize goals. A model is proposed to overcome this defect.

Runge, Carlisle P., and Church, W.L. "New Directions in Regionalization: A Case Study of Intergovernmental Relations in Northwestern Wisconsin." WISCONSIN LAW REVIEW 2 (1971): 449-519.

> The authors found a lack of comprehensive and effective planning at all levels of government and a serious shortfall between planning and implementation. They urge the development of strengthened planning and coordinating agencies at the multicounty, regional, and state levels.

Sazama, Gerald W. "A Cost Benefit Analysis of a Regional Development Incentive: State Loans." JOURNAL OF REGIONAL SCIENCE 10 (1970): 385-97.

> A cost benefit model is developed and applied to analyze the impact of state industrial development loans. The author concludes that they work as an effective tool for regional development; the evaluation method is also more generally applicable.

Scott, Stanley, and Nathan, Harriet, eds. ADAPTING GOVERNMENT TO REGIONAL NEEDS. Berkeley and Los Angeles: University of California, Institute of Governmental Affairs, 1971. 306 p.

> Report of a 1970 conference on San Francisco Bay Area regional organization. Participants describe the status of regional efforts and agencies. Three state legislative proposals for regional government are analyzed and compared.

Steele. "Regional Planning and Infrastructure Investments Based on Examples from Turkey." See 2.5.3 (p. 74)

Walker, David Bradstreet. "Interstate Regional Instrumentalities: A New Piece in an Old Puzzle." JOURNAL OF AMERICAN INSTITUTE OF PLANNERS 38 (November 1972): 359-68.

> An assessment of the four categories of federal multistate regional commissions established between 1961 and 1971, their collective experience, and an evaluation of their record.

2.3.4 Metropolitan and Local Planning

American Institute of Planners. Technical Seminars on State and Metropolitan Planning. IMPROVING STATE AND METROPOLITAN PLANNING: PLANNING PROGRAM MANAGEMENT, URBAN DEVELOPMENT COSTS. Washington, D.C.: 6 and 7 January 1969. 124 p.

> Includes "A 'Total' Look at Comprehensive Metropolitan Planning" (Hansen), "Agency Management in the Twin Cities" (Einsweiler), "State Planning: Some Issues in Developing a Work Program" (Spader), and "Urban Development Cost Analysis and State Planning" (Slavin).

Blumstein, James F., and Walter, Benjamin, eds. GROWING METROPOLIS: ASPECTS OF DEVELOPMENT IN NASHVILLE. Nashville, Tenn.: Vanderbilt University Press, 1975. 364 p.

> A compendium of papers by members of the Vanderbilt faculty, which includes contributions on the politics of zoning and development and the budget as a steering device (Salamon and Wamsley), federal aid and local government (Rondinelli and Davis), and a case study of Nashville Model Cities (Gates et al). Other chapters deal with physical, demographic, and economic aspects of the Nashville metropolis.

Bosselman, Fred P. "The Local Planner's Role Under the Proposed Model Land Development Code." JOURNAL OF AMERICAN INSTITUTE OF PLANNERS 41 (January 1975): 15-20.

> A review of the local planning implications of the American Law Institute's proposed model code, which proposes to offer incentives for local planning rather than mandating planning activity.

Boyce, David E.; Day, Norman D.; and McDonald, Chris. METROPOLITAN PLAN MAKING: AN ANALYSIS OF EXPERIENCE WITH THE PREPARATION AND EVALUATION OF ALTERNATIVE LAND USE AND TRANSPORTATION PLANS. Monograph Series No. 4. Philadelphia: Regional Science Research Institute, 1970. 475 p. Paperbound.

> Part 1 of this book presents a general review of metropolitan planning concepts and experience in seven metropolitan areas (Baltimore, Boston, Chicago, Milwaukee, Twin Cities, New York, and Philadelphia), including the formulation and evaluation of alternatives. The authors conclude that, as formulated, the alternatives were too similar for effective evaluation. In part 2 they present their recommendations for overcoming this difficulty, mainly by replacing the typical goal-oriented planning process by a cyclical planning process including the development of goals.

Brown, F. Gerald, and Murphy, Thomas P., eds. EMERGING PATTERNS IN URBAN ADMINISTRATION. Lexington, Mass.: D.C. Heath, 1970. 196 p.

> A collection of papers on various aspects of urban administration and local government; of interest are contributions dealing with the administration of local and metropolitan planning agencies.

Cowling. SUB-REGIONAL PLANNING STUDIES. See 2.5.2 (p. 69)

Finney, Graham S. "The Intergovernmental Context of Local Planning." In PRINCIPLES AND PRACTICE OF URBAN PLANNING, edited by William I. Goodman and Eric C. Freund, pp. 29-48. Washington, D.C.: International City Managers' Association, 1968. 621 p.

> The author addresses the problems of multiple jurisdictions and levels of government as they affect planners in local government. Current corrective efforts are reviewed, including structural changes at the federal and state levels and the diffusion of PPBS.

Frisken, Frances. "The Metropolis and the Central City: Can One Government Unite Them?" URBAN AFFAIRS QUARTERLY 8 (June 1973): 385-422.

> This paper examines recent proposals and innovations designed to stimulate coordinated metropolitan policy making in the light of recent trends. Illustrated by a case study of the Northeast Ohio Areawide Coordinating Agency in the Cleveland metropolitan area.

Getter, Russell W., and Elliot, Nick. "Receptivity of Local Elites Toward Planning." JOURNAL OF AMERICAN INSTITUTE OF PLANNERS 42 (January 1976): 87-95.

> Based on a survey of 1,177 board members in 71 Wisconsin counties, the authors develop a predictive model to analyze officials' support of the planning function. They find that environmental factors prove to be better predictors of receptivity than officials' personal and political characteristics.

Goldfield, David R. "Historic Planning and Redevelopment in Minneapolis." JOURNAL OF AMERICAN INSTITUTE OF PLANNERS 42 (January 1976): 76-86.

> A description and analysis of the city's planning and redevelopment efforts, focusing on the role of the private sector. The author concludes that this experience demonstrates the benefits of public-private cooperation and of a historical perspective in the planning process.

Gordon, Diana R. CITY LIMITS: BARRIERS TO CHANGE IN URBAN GOVERNMENT. New York: Charterhouse, 1973. 329 p.

> The genesis, planning, and implementation of six programs in New York City are described and analyzed. The author concludes that the bureaucratic rigidities of large city administrations are serious barriers to positive change, and that local governments can only effect such changes if they are following external societal trends.

Heikoff, Joseph M. "Economic Analysis and Metropolitan Organization." (With Commentary by Robert L. Bish.) JOURNAL OF AMERICAN INSTITUTE OF PLANNERS 39 (November 1973): 402-12.

> A critique of public choice theory as applied to fiscal policy at the local government level. Reference is made particularly to Robert L. Bish's THE PUBLIC ECONOMY OF METROPOLITAN AREAS (Chicago: Markham, 1971), which the author attacks for its market assumptions and efficiency criteria. Bish replies that Heikoff's criticism is based on a misunderstanding of public choice theory.

Hirsch, Werner Z., and Sonenblum, Sidney, eds. GOVERNING URBAN AMERICA IN THE 1970'S. New York: Praeger, 1973. 203 p.

> Includes "Evaluating Governance" (Sonenblum), "Interest Group Power and American Democracy" (Ries), "Giant Governments and Centralized Power" (Hirsch), "The Land Use Planning and Zoning Game" (Hagman et al), and "Organizing for Political Change" (Halpern).

Howard, John T. "The Local Planning Agency: Internal Administration." In PRINCIPLES AND PRACTICE OF URBAN PLANNING, edited by William I. Goodman and Eric C. Freund, pp. 546-63. Washington, D.C.: International City Managers' Association, 1968. 621 p.

> Mandatory and optional activities are identified, and definitions are offered of long-, middle-, and short-range planning. Other administration issues include the organization and allocation of work, programming and budgeting, staff management, and office procedures. A pragmatic nuts-and-bolts approach useful to the beginning administrator.

Jacobson and Prakash. METROPOLITAN GROWTH. See 2.5.3 (p. 72)

Jefferson, Ray. "Planning and the Innovation Process." In PROGRESS IN PLANNING, edited by D.R. Diamond and J.B. McLoughlin. Vol. 1, pp. 233-312. Oxford: Pergamon Press, 1973.

> A survey of 133 local planning agencies in Great Britain provided data for this analysis of innovativeness in adoption of new planning methods and procedures. Factors contributing to innovativeness are identified, and the author recommends changes in the planning environments.

Krumholz, Norman, et al. "The Cleveland Policy Planning Report." JOURNAL OF AMERICAN INSTITUTE OF PLANNERS 41 (September 1975): 298-304.

> A description of the goals and process of developing the Cleveland policy plan by its major participants. The report is unique because it is not framed in traditional planning terms but is a catalog of action recommendations. The authors develop conclusions from their experience on the roles of professional competence, taking initiative, and political involvement in the success of their efforts, and suggest some changes in the roles of the local planner.

McDowell, Bruce D., and Mindlin, Albert. "Obtaining Metropolitan Planning Data from Local Governments." JOURNAL OF AMERICAN INSTITUTE OF PLANNERS 37 (March 1971): 111-15.

> Presents an automated land use data system developed by the Metropolitan Washington Council of Governments (COG).

Meltsner, Arnold J., and Wildavsky, Aaron. "Leave City Budgeting Alone." In FINANCING THE METROPOLIS; PUBLIC POLICY IN URBAN ECONOMIES, edited by John P. Crecine, pp. 311-62. Urban Affairs Annual Review, vol. 4. Beverly Hills, Calif.: Sage, 1970.

> Important decisions are not made by planners in local government, because planning is the allocation of values. It is proposed to make the mayor's or city manager's office the client for planning proposals, and to integrate them with policy analysis. Retention of the traditional budgeting system and its association with policy analysis is advocated.

Needleman, Martin L., and Needleman, Carolyn Emerson. GUERRILLAS IN THE BUREAUCRACY: THE COMMUNITY PLANNING EXPERIMENT IN THE UNITED STATES. New York: Wiley, 1974. 368 p.

> The authors analyze the development of community planning experiments in six major cities, based on interviews with participants. They discovered an inherent conflict between these programs and the goals and organization of their parent local planning bureaucracies. Involved planners respond by becoming administrative

guerrillas, but to the extent that they and their programs are effective, they polarize the planning department and city administration. The implications are drawn of this experiment for decentralized planning as an approach to guiding city development.

Pickford, James H. "The Local Planning Agency: Organization and Structure."
In PRINCIPLES AND PRACTICE OF URBAN PLANNING, edited by William I.
Goodman and Eric C. Freund, pp. 523-40. Washington, D.C.: International
City Managers' Association, 1968. 621 p.

The local planning agency is put into its governmental context,
and its evolution and functions are discussed. Four typical patterns
of organization are identified: the independent planning commission,
the planning department, the community development department,
and the administrative planning agency. These are analyzed, and
functional and internal organization is discussed. Finally, the
author addresses the problems of agency relationships with its external environment.

Rabinovitz. CITY POLITICS AND BUREAUCRACY. See 2.2.2 (p. 37)

Ranney, David C. PLANNING AND POLITICS IN THE METROPOLIS. Columbus, Ohio: Charles E. Merrill, 1969. 179 p. Paperbound.

A concise review of planning in the metropolitan context, focusing
on intergovernmental relations. While lacking depth, it is a useful overview.

Rogers, David. THE MANAGEMENT OF BIG CITIES: INTEREST GROUPS
AND SOCIAL CHANGE STRATEGIES. Beverly Hills, Calif.: Sage, 1971.
189 p.

A study of the power structures and bureaucratic interactions connected with program planning and implementation in New York,
Philadelphia, and Cleveland. The focus is on the institutional
obstacles to innovation and change, which are pointedly illustrated
in a series of cases. The author's conclusions are pessimistic about
the potential for change.

Rose, Albert. GOVERNING METROPOLITAN TORONTO: A SOCIAL AND
POLITICAL ANALYSIS, 1953-1971. Berkeley and Los Angeles: University of
California Press, 1972. 201 p.

A description of the beginnings and growth of metropolitan government in Toronto, and of the troubles that confronted the metropolitan concept in execution between 1953 and 1971. The author
notes the physical focus of metropolitan policy and the devolution
of power from the central city to the suburbs.

Schoop, E. Jack, and Hirten, John E. "The San Francisco Bay Plan: Combining Policy with Police Power." JOURNAL OF AMERICAN INSTITUTE OF PLANNERS 37 (January 1971): 2-10.

A description of plan development and implementation of the San Francisco Bay Conservation and Development Commission. The plan evolved as a series of policy decisions based on the commission's power to control bay filling and dredging.

Smith, Edward Ellis, and Riggs, Durward S., eds. LAND USE, OPEN SPACE, AND THE GOVERNMENT PROCESS: THE SAN FRANCISCO BAY AREA EXPERIENCE. New York: Praeger, 1974. 214 p.

Traces land use and development trends around San Francisco Bay and the growth of unplanned urban and suburban sprawl.

Strong, Ann L. PRIVATE PROPERTY AND THE PUBLIC INTEREST: THE BRANDYWINE EXPERIENCE. Baltimore, Md.: Johns Hopkins University Press, 1975. 206 p.

The development of a local plan for environmental management in the upper Brandywine watershed area, near Philadelphia, in which the author participated, is described. Though landowners' interests were incorporated in the plan's approach to development rights acquisition, conservative interests eroded support for the plan until its defeat. A series of recommendations are presented for local environmental planning in the future.

Szanton, Peter L. "Analysis and Urban Government: Experience of the New York City-Rand Institute." POLICY SCIENCES 3 (July 1972): 153-62.

A participant in the four years' joint planning-analysis effort describes the background and reflects on the lessons.

Walker, Robert A. THE PLANNING FUNCTION IN URBAN GOVERNMENT. 2d ed. Chicago: University of Chicago Press, 1950. 410 p.

This is a classic study examining the role of city planning in local government. The author describes the range of planning activities and several cases in his experience, and advocates making planning a staff function under the chief executive, rather than an independent commission.

Winholtz, Wilford G. "Planning and the Public." In PRINCIPLES AND PRACTICE OF URBAN PLANNING, edited by William I. Goodman and Eric C. Freund, pp. 564-82. Washington, D.C.: International City Managers' Association, 1968. 621 p.

After a plea for two-way public-planners relationships, the author identifies appropriate public-oriented activities for a local planning agency. These include appearances by the director, meetings with citizen groups, and instructions for relations with the media.

Zimmerman, Joseph F., ed. GOVERNMENT OF THE METROPOLIS: SELECTED READINGS. New York: Holt, Rinehart and Winston, 1968. 345 p. Paperbound.

> Chapters relevant to urban planning include "City and Suburb: Community of Chaos," "Metro Nashville," "Metropolitan Dade County Government: A Review of Accomplishments," "Greater London," "Limited Function Metro Government for the Bay Area," "The Metropolitan Planning Agency: A Profile," and "Who Benefits from Metropolitan Planning."

2.4 NONGOVERNMENTAL PLANNING

2.4.1 The Private Sector

Branch, Melville C. THE CORPORATE PLANNING PROCESS. New York: American Management Association, 1962. 253 p.

> An early analysis of corporate planning, focusing on the process of setting goals. A number of analytical techniques are presented, and implementation is discussed.

Cannon, J. Thomas. BUSINESS STRATEGY AND POLICY. New York: Harcourt, Brace, 1968. 573 p.

> The author describes corporate strategic planning, production, and marketing strategies, and action strategies for implementation. Using case studies as illustrations, he advocates the development of a systematic set of planning objectives for the firm to avoid the setting of fragmented and short-sighted management policy.

Collier, James R. EFFECTIVE LONG-RANGE BUSINESS PLANNING. Englewood Cliffs, N.J.: Prentice-Hall, 1968. 188 p.

> Collier dwells on the distinction between strategic corporate planning and implementation. Part 1, "Practical Considerations for Effective Planning," describes different planning approaches tailored to various specific situations. Part 2, "The Process of Long-Range Business Planning," presents analytic and organizational planning strategies and tools.

Cotton, Donald B. COMPANY-WIDE PLANNING: CONCEPT AND PROCESS. New York: Macmillan, 1970. 235 p.

> This book focuses on corporate planning as a function of top management and describes the initiation and organization of a corporate planning system and plan production.

Fisk, George, ed. THE PSYCHOLOGY OF MANAGEMENT DECISION. Lund, Sweden: Gleerup, 1967. 309 p.

Contents include "Implications of Individual Goals for Organization Theory" (Soelberg), "Human Group Model of Organization" (Haire), "Statistical Decision Theory and Cost-Benefit Analysis" (Hamburg), "Perceived and Real Organizational Behavior" (Krendel and Bloom), and "Interaction of Manager's Personality with the Environment" (Pfaff).

George, Claude S. THE HISTORY OF MANAGEMENT THOUGHT. Englewood Cliffs, N.J.: Prentice-Hall, 1968. 210 p.

The origin and development of different schools of management thought are described, and they are analyzed and compared with an equation of planning to the decision-making process.

Hilton, Peter. PLANNING CORPORATE GROWTH AND DIVERSIFICATION. New York: McGraw-Hill, 1970. 245 p.

The strategic planning process is analyzed, including anticipating change, plan definition, timing, and continuity and review. Sources of planned growth are identified: acquisition, technological change, and product innovation, and their relation to strategic planning is discussed.

INTERNATIONAL SYMPOSIUM ON LONG RANGE PLANNING. Paris, September 1965; New York: Gordon and Breach, 1967. 531 p.

Contributions include "Criteria for Planning Decisions" (Barish), "The Role of the Long Range Planner in Management" (Perrin), "Implications of a Company's Long Range Programme" (Vuillaume), "Organizing for Planning in a Large Decentralized Company" (Denning), "The Role of the Economic Consultant in Planning" (Dean), and many other contributions with a methodological orientation.

Koontz, Harold, and O'Donnell, C. MANAGEMENT: A BOOK OF READINGS. New York: McGraw-Hill, 1964. 563 p.

Includes articles on "Planning" (Fayol) and "Managerial Planning" (Goetz).

LeBreton, Preston P., and Henning, Dale A. PLANNING THEORY. Englewood Cliffs, N.J.: Prentice-Hall, 1961. 357 p.

Planning theory based on the rational planning model is presented with a focus on business and managerial applications. Planning is involved in all phases of corporate enterprise: organization, control, coordination, staffing, and direction.

Lightwood, Martha B. PUBLIC AND BUSINESS PLANNING IN THE UNITED STATES: A BIBLIOGRAPHY. Management Information Guide No. 26. Detroit: Gale Research, 1972. 309 p.

Notable for her review of the functional aspects of business planning: economic, managerial and organization, financial, research
and development, manufacturing production and plant location,
market planning, business forecasts, and manpower planning.

Scott, Brian W. LONG RANGE PLANNING IN AMERICAN INDUSTRY.
New York: American Manufacturing Association, 1965. 288 p.

An introduction to business long-range planning and a description
of its nature. Covers its tenets, corporate evaluation, establishing
objectives, and closes with some assumptions about the organization needed for future long-range planning, and its implications
for top management.

Steiner, George A. TOP MANAGEMENT PLANNING. New York: Macmillan, 1969. 795 p.

Part 1 addresses the fundamentals of planning and presents models
of the corporate planning process, emphasizing the importance of
planning and management's salient role. Part 2 describes the
process of plan development and operationalization. Part 3 discusses rational decision making and reviews basic decision tools.
Part 4 reviews some functional areas, and part 5 illustrates problems in some cases and projects anticipated trends.

_____, ed. MANAGERIAL LONG-RANGE PLANNING. New York:
McGraw-Hill, 1963. 334 p.

Numerous cases are presented in the public and private sectors,
such as NASA in the former and Allstate Insurance in the latter.
The editor concludes from these "lessons of experience" that the
role of the manager is dominant in the planning process. This
process evolves through typical stages of development and involves standard organizational patterns. These include a central
staff group, or corporations with divisional planning staffs. Procedural planning steps are identified, and the relationship of planning staffs to other organizational units is analyzed.

Steiner, George A., and Cannon, Warren M., eds. MULTINATIONAL COR-
PORATE PLANNING. London: Macmillan and Co., 1966. 330 p.

Cases include IBM World Trade Division, Merck, and Phillips.
The environment of corporate planning is analyzed in contributions
covering national interests in general, national planning and business (including France), the Common Market, and NATO. The
book concludes with a comparison between multinational corporate
planning in the United States and in Western Europe. The authors
suggest that with the prospective increase in multinational operations, and with a sure increase in environmental complexity,
orderly corporate planning will have to become adaptable to
change.

Thompson, S. HOW COMPANIES PLAN. Research Study No. 54. New York: American Management Association, 1962. 215 p.

> A basic review of the corporate planning process is illustrated by a series of case studies.

2.4.2 Neighborhood and Community

Aleshire, Robert. "Planning and Citizen Participation: Costs, Benefits, and Approaches." URBAN AFFAIRS QUARTERLY 5 (June 1970): 369-93.

> In this evaluation of the respective advantages and costs of maximizing citizen participation in the planning process, the author concludes that the benefits far outweigh the costs. He proposes a planning process that is more decentralized to the neighborhood level.

Altshuler, Alan. COMMUNITY CONTROL: THE BLACK DEMAND FOR PARTICIPATION IN LARGE AMERICAN CITIES. New York: Pegasus Press, 1970. 216 p.

> This book presents the pros and cons of neighborhood government, including the historical context of its development, major issues, and relevant competing groups. Problems in the design of community government are analyzed.

Arnstein, Sherry R. "A Ladder of Citizen Participation." JOURNAL OF AMERICAN INSTITUTE OF PLANNERS 35 (July 1969): 216-24.

> A taxonomy of types of citizen participation at different levels of decision making. The paper focuses on an exploration of the differences between token participation or co-optation and effective policy making and control.

Blaustein, Arthur. "What is Community Economic Development?" URBAN AFFAIRS QUARTERLY 6 (September 1970): 52-70.

> A critique of the limited business and governmental efforts in ghetto economic development, and a discussion of community economic development focusing on its political aspects and the psychic benefits of participation.

Blecher, Earl M. ADVOCACY PLANNING FOR URBAN DEVELOPMENT. New York: Praeger, 1971. 180 p.

> Six neighborhood planning programs are analyzed and evaluated in terms of two variables: their professional staff and their organizational structure. They fall into three basic types: professionalized, with contract relationship to consultant; nonprofessional, with a developed hierarchy; and professionalized, run by a strong executive board. Blecher concludes that both in the organization's

responsiveness to community needs and in terms of effectiveness of service, the professional-contract model worked best.

Bryant, Coralie, and White, Louise G. "The Calculus of Competing Goals: Planning Participation and Social Change." GROWTH AND CHANGE 6 (January 1975): 38-43.

A case study of planning in a community organization--the Model Inner City Community Organization of Washington, D.C.--illustrates the conflict between the rhetoric and realities of participative planning.

Cloward, Richard A., and Elman, Richard M. "Advocacy in the Ghetto." TRANS-ACTION 4 (December 1966): 27-35.

A description of the Mobilization for Youth Program on the Lower East Side of New York, including an evaluation of its impacts after four years of activity.

Ford Foundation. COMMUNITY DEVELOPMENT CORPORATIONS: A STRATEGY FOR DEPRESSED URBAN AND RURAL AREAS. New York: Ford Foundation, May 1973. 30 p. Paperbound.

This policy paper presents the history of the CDC concept and the rationale for CDCs as a community development tool, and offers profiles of selected CDCs.

Gilbert, Neil. CLIENTS OR CONSTITUENTS: COMMUNITY ACTION IN THE WAR ON POVERTY. San Francisco: Jossey-Bass, 1970. 192 p.

A case study of poverty action programs in Pittsburgh, 1964-67. The author concludes that failures were due to structural constraints which inhibited collective action and to divisions of loyalty among the professional leadership.

Godschalk, David R. PARTICIPATION, PLANNING AND EXCHANGE IN OLD AND NEW COMMUNITIES: A COLLABORATIVE PARADIGM. Chapel Hill: Center for Urban and Regional Studies, University of North Carolina, 1972. 318 p. Paperbound.

Godschalk, after a review of citizen participation studies and models, offers his own paradigm of participative planning, consisting of a collaborative exchange between planners and citizens, a barter of responsiveness for support. Reston and Columbia, as new communities, and Levittown, West Oakland, and North Philadelphia are analyzed in terms of this model. The author concludes with some predictions on the future of participative planning and advocates adoption of his model.

Greenstone, T. David, and Peterson, Paul E. RACE AND AUTHORITY IN

URBAN POLITICS: COMMUNITY PARTICIPATION AND THE WAR ON POVER-
TY. New York: Russell Sage Foundation, 1973. 364 p.

> This analysis of community action programs in Philadelphia, New
> York, Chicago, Detroit, and Los Angeles focuses on institutional
> racism as a determinant of outcomes. The authors conclude that
> community control can be an internal objective of black organiza-
> tions, but that it is not the appropriate approach for the achieve-
> ment of equality.

Hallman, Howard W. NEIGHBORHOOD CONTROL OF PUBLIC PROGRAMS:
CASE STUDIES OF COMMUNITY CORPORATIONS AND NEIGHBORHOOD
BOARDS. New York: Praeger, 1970. 226 p.

> A survey of thirty community organizations, focusing on the relation-
> ship between participation and their effectiveness in goals achieve-
> ment. Hallman concludes that efficiency criteria are misplaced in
> this context, and that the movement towards community control
> should be viewed in a long range perspective.

Hampden-Turner, Charles. FROM POVERTY TO DIGNITY: A STRATEGY FOR
POOR AMERICANS. Garden City, N.Y.: Anchor-Doubleday, 1974. 300 p.

> A planning and development strategy for poor and ghetto communi-
> ties is presented, focusing on community development corporations and
> including descriptions and evaluations of existing CDCs. The ap-
> pendix detailing selected characteristics of a sample of CDCs is
> especially useful.

Kaplan, Marshall. "Advocacy and Urban Planning." In THE SOCIAL WEL-
FARE FORUM, published for the National Conference on Social Welfare, pp.
58-77. New York: Columbia University Press, 1968.

> A review of the history of the advocacy planning concept, fol-
> lowed by the premises underlying its evolution. The role of advo-
> cacy planning is defined through an exploration of a case in West
> Oakland.

Kramer, Ralph M. PARTICIPATION OF THE POOR: COMPARATIVE COM-
MUNITY CASE STUDIES IN THE WAR ON POVERTY. Englewood Cliffs, N.J.:
Prentice-Hall, 1969. 273 p.

> Based on detailed case studies of community organizations in San
> Francisco, Santa Clara, Oakland, Berkeley, and Contra Costa
> County (California), Kramer classifies three types of response to
> the citizen participation mandate: "debate," "game," and "fight."
> He concludes that community organizations face a difficult choice
> between accountability, service delivery, and organizational main-
> tenance. Autonomous neighborhood corporations are, according
> to Kramer, the next step.

Marris, Peter, and Rein, Martin. DILEMMAS OF SOCIAL REFORM. New York: Atherton Press, 1967. 248 p.

> Describes the development of the Ford Foundation Gray Areas Program and other precursors of the Community Action Program. The early experience of CAP is reviewed, focusing on issues of planning, comprehensive coordination of services, and participation. Ends with a tentative upbeat conclusion.

Maziotti, Donald F. "The Underlying Assumptions of Advocacy Planning: Pluralism and Reform." (With commentary by Paul and Linda Davidoff.) JOURNAL OF AMERICAN INSTITUTE OF PLANNERS 40 (January 1974): 38-48.

> A radical critique of the pluralist and reformist assumptions behind the advocacy planning model in theory and application. The author claims that concentration of political and economic power and limited access to decision making put these assumptions in question. The Davidoffs in their commentary agree with some of these points but suggest that this model is one avenue for reform through the existing systems.

Miller, Kenneth H. "Community Organizations in the Ghetto." In SOCIAL INNOVATION IN THE CITY: NEW ENTERPRISES FOR COMMUNITY DEVELOPMENT, edited by Richard S. Rosenbloom and Robin Marris, pp. 97-108. Cambridge, Mass.: Harvard University Press, 1969.

> Case studies and evaluations of several ghetto community development organizations.

Miller, S.M., and Rein, Martin. "Participation, Poverty and Administration." PUBLIC ADMINISTRATION REVIEW 29 (January-February 1969): 15-25.

> The impact of the participation movement on professional public administrators is analyzed. Conflicts are predicted in defining the boundaries between professional and board decisions, and the possibility of an upsurge in nepotism in hiring is discussed.

Needleman. GUERRILLAS IN THE BUREAUCRACY. See 2.3.4 (p. 55)

Peattie, Liza R. "Reflections on Advocacy Planning." JOURNAL OF AMERICAN INSTITUTE OF PLANNERS 34 (March 1968): 80-88.

> An evaluation of advocacy planning in practice which concludes that citizen participation groups again tend to represent local vested interests and not the most underprivileged.

Peterson, Paul E. "Forms of Representation: Participation of the Poor in the Community Action Program." AMERICAN POLITICAL SCIENCE REVIEW 64 (June 1970): 471-91.

A model is developed distinguishing between formal, descriptive, substantive, and interest types of representation, and it is applied to analyze cases in Chicago, Philadelphia, and New York. The author concludes that selection was a function of competing political resources and influence was affected by social orientations, which also affected the level of intraneighborhood conflict.

Piven, Frances Fox, et al. "Symposium: Whom Does the Advocate Planner Serve?" SOCIAL POLICY 1 (May-June 1970): 32-37.

Five contributors debate the question, in retrospect, of who the actual clients of advocate planners are. They include Paul and Linda Davidoff, who see advocacy planning as fulfilling its basic purposes, Chester W. Hartman, Clarence Funnye, and Frances Fox Piven, who occupy a spectrum of increasingly critical views.

Skjei, Stephen S. "Urban Systems Advocacy." JOURNAL OF AMERICAN INSTITUTE OF PLANNERS 37 (January 1972): 11-24.

An analysis of the planner's role in the debate on the decentralization of education in New York City. The author concludes that the advocacy analogy is misplaced in the context of public debate, and that the potential of advocacy planning to improve the information available to policymakers is limited.

Spiegel, Hans, ed. CITIZEN PARTICIPATION IN URBAN DEVELOPMENT. 2 vols. Washington, D.C.: Center for Community Affairs of the National Institute of Applied Behavioral Science, 1968.

Volume 1 discusses "Concepts and Issues" of public participation and reviews the development and application of the concept. Volume 2 deals with "Cases and Programs" and presents examples of public participation (pre-1967).

Vosburgh, William W., and Hyman, Drew. "Advocacy and Bureaucracy: The Life and Times of a Decentralized Advocacy Program." ADMINISTRATIVE SCIENCE QUARTERLY 18 (December 1973): 433-48.

The case of the "Governor's Branch Offices" (GBOs) in Pennsylvania, 1968-71, is analyzed. The authors conclude that there is an irresolvable conflict between decentralized advocacy and a centralized bureaucracy.

Weissman, Harold H. COMMUNITY COUNCILS AND COMMUNITY CONTROL: THE WORKINGS OF DEMOCRATIC MYTHOLOGY. Pittsburgh: University of Pittsburgh Press, 1970. 214 p.

The results of a year's study of a community council in New York's Lower East Side are put into the context of an exchange model developed by the author. This model includes both material and psychic rewards, and he shows how their effective utilization leads to community control over the program.

Yates, Douglas. "Neighborhood Government." POLICY SCIENCES 3 (July 1972): 209-17.

> An analysis of the obstacles and advantages of neighborhood government, which concludes that while it is a desirable goal, its potential is limited.

2.5 PLANNING ABROAD AND COMPARATIVE STUDIES

2.5.1 Comparative Planning Studies

Bor, Walter. THE MAKING OF CITIES. London: Leonard Hill, 1972. 256 p.

> The author analyzes the techniques of planning and their respective political environments in the United States and Great Britain. Planning applications are seen as responses to current urban problems, with a focus on the design of the urban environment. Detailed attention is given to housing and transportation issues, and numerous examples of applications, from a wide range of countries, illustrate the author's propositions.

Bunker, Raymond. TOWN AND COUNTRY OR CITY AND REGION? Melbourne: Melbourne University Press, 1971. 164 p.

> This book examines changes in selected large cities since 1945, physical planning operations in these cities, and relates them to emerging planning models. The cases include planning and administration in Great Britain, the United States, Canada, and Australia, with detailed studies of Washington, D.C., Chicago, London, New York, Toronto, and Sydney.

Clawson, Marion, and Hall, Peter. PLANNING AND URBAN GROWTH: AN ANGLO-AMERICAN COMPARISON. Baltimore, Md.: Johns Hopkins University Press, 1973. xii, 300 p.

> Urban land development and planning in Great Britain and the United States are studied in a comparison which points out the results of planning and nonplanning since World War II. The Northeastern Urban Complex in the United States and Southeast England, with special focus on the metropolises of New York and London, are analyzed in detail. The comparison shows that the British system of elaborate planning and the U.S. system of nonplanning are surprisingly similar in their outputs: urban environments which were not the result of any conscious public choice.

Friedly, Philip H. NATIONAL POLICY RESPONSES TO URBAN GROWTH. Lexington, Mass.: D.C. Heath, 1975. 221 p.

> A review of innovative growth control strategies and major policy attitudes of selected countries in Western Europe and North America.

Friedly applies analytical models to detail the shift from traditional regional development policies to present urban growth management approaches. His evaluation of policy innovations is useful.

Hoffman, George W. REGIONAL DEVELOPMENT STRATEGIES IN SOUTHEAST
EUROPE: A COMPARATIVE ANALYSIS OF ALBANIA, BULGARIA, GREECE,
ROMANIA, AND YUGOSLAVIA. New York: Praeger, 1972. xx, 322 p.

Using a historical approach combined with his own field experience, the author analyzes trends since World War II. He highlights the conflict between economic rationality and political ex-
pediency as the ongoing dilemma of regional development.

Ostrowski, Waclaw. CONTEMPORARY TOWN PLANNING: PRESENT TRENDS.
Translated by Doris Ronowicz and Jadwiga Przybylska. The Hague: International Federation for Housing and Planning, 1973. 682 p. Paperbound.

An overview of urban planning in the developed world, both socialist and mixed economies. The author is optimistic about the
achievements and prospects for urban planning and responds ag-
gressively to critics of the profession. The book is organized
along functional categories: central cities, residential, industry,
recreation, and so forth. Ostrowski concludes by identifying the
necessary conditions for successful planning: they include adequate land reserves, influence on development processes, adequate
funding, and social commitment to the planning activity.

Rodwin, Lloyd. NATIONS AND CITIES: A COMPARISON OF STRATEGIES
FOR URBAN GROWTH. Boston: Houghton-Mifflin, 1970. xvi, 395 p.

Case studies of national planning and control of urbanization in
Turkey, Venezuela, Great Britain, France, and the United States
lead to conclusions on the type and possibility of an optimal
growth management policy in the United States.

United Nations. Department of Economic and Social Affairs. URBANIZATION
IN THE SECOND UNITED NATIONS DEVELOPMENT DECADE. New York:
1970. 39 p. Paperbound.

A review of historic and contemporary causes and effects of urban
growth, and proposals for some approaches to the urban crisis.
Urbanization strategies are identified for inclusion in national
priorities and in the international goals to be adopted at the
forthcoming (1972) Stockholm U.N. Conference on the Human
Environment.

Walsh, Annemarie H. THE URBAN CHALLENGE TO GOVERNMENT: AN
INTERNATIONAL COMPARISON OF THIRTEEN CITIES. New York: Praeger,
1969. 294 p.

A study comparing diverse cities, such as Calcutta, Lagos, Leningrad, Lima, Stockholm, Toronto, Valencia, and Zagreb, on various aspects of the urban environment and government, including metropolitan organization and planning.

2.5.2 Planning in Developed Countries

Abrams, Irwin, and Francaviglia, Richard. "Urban Planning in Poland Today." JOURNAL OF AMERICAN INSTITUTE OF PLANNERS 41 (July 1975): 258–69.

A review of the aims and accomplishments of Polish urban planning over the last thirty years. These include postwar urban reconstruction, historic conservation, a planned settlement network, integrated physical–economic planning, and attention to environmental protection.

Adizes, Ichak. INDUSTRIAL DEMOCRACY: YUGOSLAV STYLE. THE EFFECT OF DECENTRALIZATION ON ORGANIZATIONAL BEHAVIOR. New York: Free Press, 1971. 297 p.

The Yugoslav experiment in participatory planning and decentralized management is described and evaluated. The author offers a balanced estimate of the merits and limitations of this system.

Akzin, Benjamin, and Dror, Yehezkel. ISRAEL: HIGH PRESSURE PLANNING. Syracuse, N.Y.: Syracuse University Press, 1966. 90 p.

Akzin and Dror analyze the planning process in Israel, primarily at the national level, and conclude that it is an example of what they call "facet planning": planning in depth in individual sectors with little integration between them. The authors see this as an effective response to critical short-range problems, but predict problems for long-range planning under this sytem.

Altman, Elizabeth A., and Rosenbaum, Betsey R. "Principles of Planning and Zionist Ideology." JOURNAL OF AMERICAN INSTITUTE OF PLANNERS 39 (September 1973): 316–25.

This article outlines the influence of Zionist ideology on national planning strategies in Israel. The experience of development towns is analyzed, leading to the conclusion that, while ideology can prescribe course of action, implementation and its constraints force compromises, since socioeconomic characteristics are too complex for simplistic goals.

Cohen, Stephen S. MODERN CAPITALIST PLANNING: THE FRENCH MODEL. Cambridge, Mass.: Harvard University Press, 1969. 310 p.

The development and impacts of French national planning are traced out in detail, with special attention to the relations between the planning bureaucracy and its political and corporate environment. The author's assessment is that the apparently effective results of French planning are largely due to its limited aspirations.

Cooper, Colin; Howel, Brandon; and Lyddon, Derek. "Regional Planning and Implementation." JOURNAL OF THE TOWN PLANNING INSTITUTE 56 (1970): 325-31.

Three contributions, each dealing separately with Southeast England, Scotland, and Wales. The authors conclude that effective regional planning needs more compatibility between regions, more standardized methodologies, and better criteria for regional delineation.

Cowling, T.M., and Steeley, G.C. SUB-REGIONAL PLANNING STUDIES: AN EVALUATION. Oxford: Pergamon Press, 1973. 202 p.

The authors review the extensive body of subregional planning studies executed in Great Britain. Their analysis covers the topics, techniques, goals and objectives, strategy generation, evaluation, monitoring, and implementation of these efforts.

Cullingworth, J.B. PROBLEMS OF AN URBAN SOCIETY. Vol. 1: THE SOCIAL FRAMEWORK OF PLANNING. London: Allen and Unwin, 1973. 171 p.

This volume covers the demographic, social, economic, and physical characteristics of Great Britain which are the relevant framework for planning activities. Special detail is devoted to traffic and land values.

_____. PROBLEMS OF AN URBAN SOCIETY. Vol. 2: THE SOCIAL CONTEXT OF PLANNING. London: Allen and Unwin, 1973. 191 p.

The point of departure of this companion volume is the problem of poverty. Here Cullingworth describes and analyzes the context of policy development in the areas of housing, slum clearance, and race relations. British social planning efforts and public participation are given attention.

_____. TOWN AND COUNTRY PLANNING IN BRITAIN. 6th ed. London: Allen and Unwin, 1976. 287 p.

The evolution of planning and its legislative and organizational context. Other topics include land values and amenity, new and expanded towns, urban renewal, and regional planning.

Evans, Hazel, ed. NEW TOWNS: THE BRITISH EXPERIENCE. New York: Wiley, 1972. 196 p.

A comprehensive overview of the planning and implementation of the British new towns is presented in essays by participants and observers. The historical background is covered in an introductory chapter; other chapters are "Administrative Framework," "Regional and Economic Planning," "The Planning of New Towns," and "New Towns to Live In." A useful, annotated bibliography is included.

Gertler, Leonard O. REGIONAL PLANNING IN CANADA. Montreal: Harvest House, 1972. 186 p.

The book develops the following nine "themes": a philosophy of Canadian regional planning, urban impact on the agricultural hinterland, provincial and federal policies and programs, regional planning as an export to developing countries, and four regional planning projects. The focus is on macroscale regional economic development, and the book offers useful lessons for U.S. practice.

_____, ed. PLANNING THE CANADIAN ENVIRONMENT. Montreal: Harvest House, 1968. 311 p.

Papers covering "The Evolution of Planning in Canada," "The Background Ideas," "Land as Resource and Space," "Developing and Planning the Regions," and "Perspectives for Regional Planning."

Sharon, Arieh. PLANNING JERUSALEM: THE MASTER PLAN FOR THE OLD CITY OF JERUSALEM AND ITS ENVIRONS. New York: McGraw-Hill, 1973. 211 p.

The first seven chapters present relevant data about the Jerusalem area, including its history and architectural features. The second part of the book presents the planning proposals and design guidelines. In the final section, specific projects are described; these include the reconstruction of the Jewish Quarter and the Jerusalem National Park. The major contributions of this book are its historical account and analytical surveys.

2.5.3 Development Planning and the Third World

Benveniste. THE POLITICS OF EXPERTISE. See 2.2.2 (p. 34)

Caiden, Naomi, and Wildavsky, Aaron. PLANNING AND BUDGETING IN POOR COUNTRIES. New York: Wiley, 1974. 369 p.

This survey of national planning efforts in a number of developing countries includes a trenchant attack on many of the accepted dogmas of planning. The authors conclude that in the uncertain environment of poor countries attempts at comprehensive national planning are misplaced, and they recommend a more incremental, project-oriented approach. A valuable addition to the descriptive literature on planning, exposing the relations between planning,

budgeting, political power, and implementation, without conceal-
ing the authors' own biases.

California. University of, Los Angeles. Committee on International and Com-
parative Studies. SECOND ANNUAL SPRING COLLOQUIUM ON COM-
PARATIVE URBANIZATION--PROCEEDINGS. NEW CONCEPTS AND TECH-
NOLOGIES IN THIRD WORLD URBANIZATION. Los Angeles: University of
California, School of Architecture and Urban Planning, 1974. 238 p.

> Includes "Rural Development Programs" (Ruttan), "Chinese Experi-
> ments in Urban Space" (Satter), "New Towns" (Mittelbach), and
> "Education and Development in Urbanizing Societies" (Hudson).

Catanese, Anthony James. "Frustrations of National Planning: Reality and
Theory in Colombia." JOURNAL OF AMERICAN INSTITUTE OF PLANNERS
39 (March 1973): 93-105.

> The development of national planning in Colombia is described
> and analyzed, with special attention to the relations between the
> planner-technocrats, bureaucrats, and political administrations.
> The author concludes that planning is too narrowly focused on
> technical methodologies and that planning methods should be
> adopted which are more relevant to the political and social con-
> text.

Daland, Robert T. BRAZILIAN PLANNING: DEVELOPMENT, POLITICS, AND
ADMINISTRATION. Chapel Hill: University of North Carolina Press, 1967.
231 p.

> A history and analysis of planning in Brazil, focusing on the na-
> tional economic and physical planning efforts of the mid-sixties
> under the Kubitschek and Goulart administrations, and the sub-
> sequent transition to the military regime. The author concludes
> from this Brazilian experience that, in an unstable political sys-
> tem, central planning is a response to the political maintenance
> needs of the regime, but that central planning, in such a context,
> is perceived as disfunctional by most actors if it tries to intervene
> in the existing bureaucracy.

Davies, Jon Gower. THE EVANGELISTIC BUREAUCRAT: A STUDY OF A
PLANNING EXERCISE IN NEWCASTLE UPON TYNE. London: Tavistock
Publications, 1972. 239 p.

> The case of a neighborhood planning effort in the "Rye Hill" area
> of Newcastle is described and analyzed to point out the effects
> of an "urban renewal-" oriented planning ideology. In his con-
> cluding section, the author analyzes the function of planning in
> British society and questions its mandate for the adoption of the
> policies which are advocated.

Friedmann, John. "Intention and Reality: The American Planner Overseas."

JOURNAL OF AMERICAN INSTITUTE OF PLANNERS 35 (May 1969): 187-94.

> Different conditions make the training of the U.S. planner almost useless: lack of local commitment, lack of elementary data, and absence of consensual public values. American models and techniques are over-refined, and consultants lack permanence. Continuing involvement is recommended for mutual feedback between developing countries and the United States.

_____. REGIONAL DEVELOPMENT POLICY. See 2.3.3. (p.50)

_____. URBANIZATION, PLANNING, AND NATIONAL DEVELOPMENT. Beverly Hills, Calif.: Sage, 1973. 351 p.

> This book is an adapted compendium of some of the author's papers which appeared between 1966 and 1972. It presents his theory of urbanization and polarized regional development, illustrated by cases from Chile and Venezuela. Includes a brief annotated bibliography (to 1970) of development planning cases.

Gramer, Robert E. POLITICS OF URBAN DEVELOPMENT IN SINGAPORE. Ithaca, N.Y.: Cornell University Press, 1972. 263 p.

> This book opens with a description of the local background and Singapore's political and administrative context. The centerpiece is an analysis of Kallang Basin Reclamation Project and the roles of the respective actors in its development. The third part is a comparison of this planning process with other developing countries and the United States. The detailed case study is a useful addition to a rare genre.

Hirschman, Albert O. "Policymaking and Policy Analysis in Latin America: A Return Journey." POLICY SCIENCES 6 (December 1975): 385-402.

> A review and conceptual updating of the author's JOURNEYS TOWARDS PROGRESS (1963), illustrating in a Colombian example the indirect and unanticipated effects of policy. Hirschman recommends special attention to side effects.

Jacobsen, Leo, and Prakash, Ved, eds. METROPOLITAN GROWTH: PUBLIC POLICY FOR SOUTH AND SOUTHEAST ASIA. New York: Halstead Press, 1974. 258 p.

> Includes "The Measurement of Metropolitan Performance: Singapore and Bangkok as Pacemakers" (Meier), "Metropolitan Planning in Karachi: A Case Study" (Shibli), "Metropolitan Problems and Prospects--Calcutta" (Row), and "Urban Planning in the Context of a New Urbanization" (Jacobson and Prakash).

Jaguaribe, Helio. ECONOMIC AND POLITICAL DEVELOPMENT: A THEORETICAL APPROACH AND A BRAZILIAN CASE STUDY. Cambridge, Mass.:

Harvard University Press, 1968. 202 p.

An insightful analysis of planning and implementation in developing countries by a major participant in Brazil's economic planning. Jaguaribe identifies three models of political development: state capitalism, national capitalism, and developmental socialism. He identifies successful and failed examples of each model and analyzes the reasons for these outcomes. Brazil is addressed in detail.

Junghans, Karl H. "From Rural Poverty to Urban Misery." CERES 2 (July-August 1969): 24-28.

A rare piece of followup research on a widely applauded planning effort: India's planned urbanization around its new steel plants. Junghans traces the effect on adjacent and more distant areas of the new towns, and he concludes that there were some positive impacts, but that a rural development effort is also needed.

Kaser, Michael, and Zielinsky, Janusz G. PLANNING IN EASTERN EUROPE. London: Bodley Head, 1970. 184 p.

With a focus on national economic planning, this book reviews the politics of control in Eastern European nations and develops the historic background to centralized planning there. The planning process is discussed, covering its horizons, targets, price formulation, and directive finance. Finally, the authors analyze plan implementation in these countries through the management and workers of public enterprise.

LaPalombara, Joseph. ITALY--THE POLITICS OF PLANNING. Syracuse, N.Y.: University of Syracuse Press, 1966. 184 p.

An analysis of Italian national economic planning and administration, focusing on the political context.

Manners, Gerald, et al. REGIONAL DEVELOPMENT IN GREAT BRITAIN. New York: Wiley, 1972. 448 p.

This study analyzes regional economic change in Great Britain's "standard economic regions," focusing on the impacts of regional policy, especially decisions resulting from consumer pressures and political interests. The authors highlight the importance of regional policy by pointing out how pervasive its impacts are.

Meier, Richard L. DEVELOPMENTAL PLANNING. New York: McGraw-Hill, 1965. 420 p.

Meier presents an integrated conceptual model of the development planning process, based on the concept of development as differentiation and social change. The organizational aspects of development planning are his focus, and the precepts are illustrated with cases, including a detailed review of the Puerto Rican "Operation Bootstrap" experience.

_____. PLANNING FOR AN URBAN WORLD: THE DESIGN OF RESOURCE CONSERVING CITIES. Cambridge: MIT Press, 1974. 515 p.

In this monumental work, Meier summarizes his research on the developmental characteristics of cities, the processes of urbanization and social change, and the planning implications of resource constraints on the one hand and technological tools on the other. His conclusions draw on an encyclopedic range of knowledge ranging from information theory to organic chemistry.

Rodwin, Lloyd, and Associates. PLANNING URBAN GROWTH AND REGIONAL DEVELOPMENT: THE EXPERIENCE OF THE GUYANA PROGRAM OF VENEZUELA. Cambridge: MIT Press, 1969. 524 p.

The planning, development, and first stages of implementation of the new city of Ciudad Guayana are described and analyzed by participants. They include members of the Harvard-MIT Joint Center for Urban Studies, who acted as planning consultants, and Venezuelan officials and administrators. This study is unique in its time span and its linkages between planning and implementation; a case study is presented in fascinating detail.

Rose. GOVERNING METROPOLITAN TORONTO. See 2.3.4 (p. 56)

Shachar, Arie S. "Israel's Development Towns: Evaluation of National Urbanization Policy." JOURNAL OF AMERICAN INSTITUTE OF PLANNERS 37 (November 1971): 362-72.

This evaluation of Israel's urbanization policy over twenty years identifies national goals and considers their effect on urbanization patterns. The derivation of planning principles from theoretical frameworks is described, and the paper concludes that while the "population dispersal" policy has succeeded, there has been a failure to achieve regional integration which should be the goal for future policy.

Shafer, Robert J. MEXICO: MUTUAL ADJUSTMENT PLANNING. Syracuse, N.Y.: Syracuse University Press, 1966. 214 p.

A description and analysis of Mexican national planning, which is based primarily on bargaining between the public and private sectors of this mixed economy.

Steele, David. "Regional Planning and Infrastructure Investment Based on Examples from Turkey." URBAN STUDIES 8 (1971): 5-20.

Turkish cases are generalized to show that industrial location decisions in developing countries can be affected by infrastructure investments, but that these must be substantial and well timed. The need for concentration of resources is emphasized.

Stolper, Wolfgang F. PLANNING WITHOUT FACTS: LESSONS IN RESOURCE ALLOCATION FROM NIGERIA'S DEVELOPMENT. Cambridge, Mass.: Harvard University Press, 1966. 348 p.

> The author's experience in Nigerian development planning is used to illustrate the limitations and methods of planning with limited information and almost no data base. He suggests decentralization and adaptability as possible solutions.

Waterston, Albert. DEVELOPMENT PLANNING: LESSONS OF EXPERIENCE. Baltimore, Md.: Johns Hopkins Press, 1965. 706 p.

> Waterston analyzes a wide range of cases of development planning, which fall into three types: project-by-project, integrated public investment planning, and comprehensive planning. The contexts are identified where each model is most suitable, and the reasons for planning failures are examined. A main conclusion is that many failures are due to a lack of political commitment, and that this is an indispensable ingredient for effective development and reform.

Wildavsky, Aaron. "Why Planning Fails in Nepal." ADMINISTRATIVE SCIENCE QUARTERLY 17 (December 1972): 508-28.

> The reasons for failure of Nepal's planning efforts are identified: they include unrealistic targets, powerlessness of the planning agency, and the political context and administrative culture of the country. Wildavsky concludes that here planning is doomed to failure, and rather than making planners more powerful, more reliance should be placed on good project analysis in a situation where interdependencies are insignificant.

Wong, John, ed. THE CITIES OF ASIA: A STUDY OF URBAN SOLUTIONS AND URBAN FINANCE. Singapore: University of Singapore Press, 1976. 450 p.

> A collection of papers presented at a 1974 international seminar, covering land use policy, urban and regional planning approaches, and revenue and taxation, in the context of Asian cities.

Wynia, Gary W. POLITICS AND PLANNERS: ECONOMIC DEVELOPMENT POLICY IN CENTRAL AMERICA. Madison: University of Wisconsin Press, 1972. 227 p.

> Based on a survey of governmental innovative planning efforts in several countries from 1965-69, Wynia concludes that efforts to apply a synoptic planning model failed. The book articulates the reasons for this failure, which include lack of commitment to this mode by the planners, political instability, and bureaucratic constraints. Included are useful detailed case histories of several projects.

Chapter 3

METHODS AND TECHNIQUES

A number of issues are raised in reviewing the literature of "planning methods." First, a number of alternative terms, though not synonymous, are often used synonymously. These include planning techniques, planning tools, planning analysis, quantitative methods of analysis, and scientific methods. Defining these terms and choosing a focus for this review was, of course, the first task undertaken.

The word "method" implies a systematic procedure--in our case, a procedure for doing planning. Also implied are the notions that these procedures are used repeatedly, have been well documented, do not vary tremendously in application, and can be taught and learned. Michael B. Tietz, in a seminal article, points out these attributes as well as the less obvious one--methods themselves are a product of societal demands. In his terms, they are themselves "social events." Thus, planning methods, as generally defined, cover the broad, possibly multistaged attack that planners mount on problems, be they social, physical, or economic; local, regional or national in scale.

Other terms are less inclusive. Planning techniques or tools most often refer to those single-stage, closed-ended procedures, often derived from the social sciences, which constitute the basis upon which most planning methodologies are built. As an example, survey research methods are a technique used in origin-destination (O-D) studies, a typical planning method employed in transportation planning. Survey research is but one of a variety of tools employed in O-D studies. Obviously, these are definitional issues, and the planner's tools may well be the sociologist's methods.

Planning analysis connotes two attributes that make it a narrower term than planning methods. First, it is often implied to be only a step in the planning process, an early step, one that involves defining the problem, gathering data, and analyzing that data. Though analysis should be done throughout the planning process, this first stage is generally implied. Second, mathematical, especially statistical, techniques are at the heart of planning analysis. Though planning methods involve many techniques of a nonmathematical nature, planning analysis seldom does. Our review includes numerous nonmathematical procedures.

Methods and Techniques

Quantitative methods are at the same time narrower and more broad. The word "method" implies, as mentioned before, a grouping of techniques, somewhat more open-ended than closed, and often multistaged. But quantitative implies that at the heart these procedures are mathematical in nature. Thus, a number of commonly used planning methods of a nonmathematical nature would be excluded from a list of quantitative methods.

Lastly, scientific methods of planning or of urban analysis imply a level of development of method which the field of planning may not yet have reached. The word "scientific" as a modifier does seem to imply a degree of closure and a level of rigor and mathematical purity which the field has not yet attained. Thus, its use could be viewed as somewhat premature.

What is implied, then, in a review of planning methods is a review of groupings of techniques and procedures in some problem-solving context. These can be aggregations of both formal and informal techniques as well as quantitative and nonquantitative ones. Having decided upon planning methods as the focus, the next issue becomes the scale of application: neighborhood, city, region, state, and national. The focus of this chapter is, by definition, methods employed in urban planning. But the word "urban" does not cleanly divide the literature of planning methods. First, there are methods used at more than one scale. A method used for regional economic analysis may well be used, adapted somewhat, for metropolitan economic analysis. Second, the next larger unit, region vis-à-vis city, or city vis-à-vis neighborhood, may provide a more complete context for the valid application of a method. To view urban areas in isolation is very often a misleading approach. For these two reasons, there is substantial spillover in the literature of urban planning from one to another.

A third issue confronting the reviewer of the methods of urban planning is how to classify the literature for the reader. Since it is the presumption of the entire volume that the reader is not usually a professional urban planner, a system had to be selected which would provide the best access to the literature for the informed lay person. Four ways of classifying the literature were examined in some detail. These included breakdowns by (1) chronological appearance and use in the planning profession and its literature; (2) disciplinary origin; (3) problem sector focus, for example, transportation; and (4) step in the planning process. All four possibilities have advantages and disadvantages, and none provides completely unambiguous, mutually exclusive categories.

Tietz listed four historical "perspectives" of planning and their associated methodologies. These perspectives are chronologically practice or craft, scientific or cognitive, social policy, and policy analysis and program evaluation. Dividing the literature using these categories raises at least two problems. First, though a methodology may have been introduced at one phase, it may have been more fully elaborated in another and had a resurgence of use in yet another. Land use law may be a case in point. Thus, to locate a particular reference, the reader would need to be rather familiar with the history of the planning profession and its methodologies. Second, given this problem, unambiguous and mutually exclusive categories are difficult to describe. Third, the typology has a pejorative air about it. The word "craft" when applied to methods in use today casts them in an unbecoming light.

Planners are eclectic. They draw their methods from a variety of disciplines and often combine many tools derived from more than one discipline into a planning method. Attempting to divide the literature by cognate field proved difficult indeed. Problems of ambiguity proved insurmountable.

Problem areas addressed by urban planners, such as housing, transportation, and land use, provide the substance upon which planning methodologies are brought to bear. Again the problems of classification are twofold. Methodologies like population projection apply to many problem areas, while multiple methodologies can be used in a single problem area. Though some methodologies have become identified with a particular substantive area, for example, models with transportation planning, it is unproductive to reinforce this stereotype.

On the face of it, dividing the literature of planning methods into steps in the planning process is even less promising. Models of the steps of the planning process that provide relatively clean categories are ordinarily normative or prescriptive in nature. In fact, a variety of scholars have found the planning process to be highly nonsequential and interactive in nature, maintaining that methodologies get used many times and really are better unlinked to any one stage. This narrower view of the planning method has produced numerous lapses in planning practice. Yet, with these caveats in mind, and with the very generalized stages designated here, the literature seems to gravitate well into unambiguous categories. These categories seem relatively accessible to the layperson.

The review of the planning methods literature has been a broad one. As in the other sections, a wide definition of urban planning has been assumed. It has gone well beyond the more restrictive definition of urban planning as intervention in the urban physical environment. To some degree the delineation of the body of literature has been tautologically derived--it is that literature which documents what planners do methodologically and the sourcebooks for how to do it. The JOURNAL OF THE AMERICAN INSTITUTE OF PLANNERS, and especially its book review section, has been an invaluable aid in this task. The citations have also been derived in part from knowing what methods are taught in schools of planning in the United States. Hopefully no basic text containing methodologies used by planners, or used in planning curricula, has been omitted.

One may view the detail of the presentations of methodologies as having several levels. First, there can be a pure description of a tool, technique, or method as it might exist in a textbook as an example. Very often citations to these volumes are derived from cognate fields. Second, there can be a demonstration of the technique and a criticism of its use in planning. And finally, there can be very detailed case studies of a methodology in use in a planning context.

Methods and Techniques

In part because books and monographs were given priority, the reader will find less material in the latter two categories. However, in addition, there simply is a paucity of methodological case material in planning. Only when periodical or fugitive material is considered "classic" or "seminal" will it be included in this bibliography.

3.1 GENERAL APPROACHES

3.1.1 Overview of Planning Methods

American Institute of Planners. JOURNAL OF THE AMERICAN INSTITUTE OF PLANNERS (special issue devoted to the science of planning) 22 (February 1956): 58-102.

> An edition of the journal which contained a number of empirical articles, including models.

Bolan, Richard S. "Emerging Views of Planning." JOURNAL OF AMERICAN INSTITUTE OF PLANNERS 33 (July 1967): 233-45.

> Bolan takes a comprehensive look, in 1967, at variations in (1) possible planning strategies, (2) possible content of planning, and (3) planning organization. He does this while at the same time looking at variations in planning method. An excellent review of the methodological "camps" at the time of the writing.

Catanese, Anthony J[ames]. SCIENTIFIC METHODS OF URBAN ANALYSIS. Urbana: University of Illinois Press, 1972. 336 p.

> Developed as an introductory text for planning students at a time when interest in systems theory and systems analysis had peaked in the planning profession. Catanese defined his area of concern as urban systems, analysis, and science. Thus, the methods displayed are (1) predictive and estimating models: matrix methods, linear models, nonlinear and probability models; (2) optimizing models: basic optimization, calculus and mathematical programming; (3) simulation and gaming; and (4) urban information systems.

Dyckman, John W. "Interpretations: The Technological Obsolescence of Planning Practice." JOURNAL OF AMERICAN INSTITUTE OF PLANNERS 27 (August 1961): 242-45.

> In this brief article, Dyckman warned practicing planners about the revolution in information (and information processing) and in scientific analysis that was about to sweep urban affairs. He noted the possible obsolescence of a field which did not keep current on the culture of science. He thus argued for the development of more sophisticated methodologies.

Greenwood, Ernest. "The Relationship of Science to the Practice Professions."
JOURNAL OF AMERICAN INSTITUTE OF PLANNERS 24 (November 1958):
223-32.

> The editor of the journal, Mel Webber, reprinted this piece ex-
> plaining that he felt that though it was aimed at the social work
> profession, it was directly relevant to planning. It makes a
> strong case for the integration of social science (and social science
> methodologies) into the practice professions.

Harris, Britton. "The Limits of Science and Humanism in Planning." JOUR-
NAL OF AMERICAN INSTITUTE OF PLANNERS 33 (September 1967): 324-35.

> A general view of science and scientific method in planning on
> the occasion of the fiftieth anniversary of the American Institute
> of Planners. The author concludes with a discussion of the capac-
> ities of science and humanism, related to the various parts of
> the planning process, suggesting a division of labor for the future.

Kaplan, Abraham B. THE CONDUCT OF INQUIRY: METHODOLOGY FOR
BEHAVIORAL SCIENCE. San Francisco: Chandler, 1964. xix, 428 p.

> This is a text which is often used in graduate planning methodology
> courses. Its thrust is the improvement of scientific methods in the
> behavioral sciences, and thus its heyday of use was a time when
> planning and behavioral science were most closely identified (the
> mid-sixties). Strong points are its discussion of problems at the
> heart of inquiry: experimentation and measurement, construction
> of models and theories, development of concepts, and discovery
> of laws.

Krueckeberg, Donald A. "Practical Demands for Planning Methods." In PLAN-
NING THEORY IN THE 1980'S, edited by R.W. Burchell and D. Listokin. New
Brunswick, N.J.: Rutgers Center for Urban Policy Research, 1978 (forthcoming).

> This is a comprehensive review of about twenty different studies
> that have examined either the use of planning methods in the
> field and/or the teaching of planning methods in graduate programs
> in planning. Discrepancies between practice and what is taught
> are discussed, and a history of planning methods is identified.

Krueckeberg, Donald A., and Silvers, Arthur L. URBAN PLANNING ANALY-
SIS: METHODS AND MODELS. New York: Wiley, 1974. xx, 486 p.

> As of this writing, this book would have to be considered the most
> widely used textbook in planning methods courses, especially
> quantitative analytic methods. Its twelve chapters largely define
> the analytic activities of planners. It is a primer in many ways.
> Well referenced, it can lead the reader to the more detailed and
> difficult material. It is used by most graduate programs in plan-
> ning as the basic text.

Methods and Techniques

Robinson, Ira. DECISION-MAKING IN URBAN PLANNING. AN INTRO-
DUCTION TO NEW METHODOLOGIES. Beverly Hills, Calif.: Sage, 1972.
628 p.

> The objective of this book was to present the "new methodologies"
> for planning which were developed in the 1960s. It is a well-
> edited reader (22 articles) which in its first section divides the
> presentation of methodologies into five categories--five stages in
> the planning process. It includes excerpts from four case studies
> which each employ some of the "new methodologies" alluded to
> in the first section.

Rondinelli, Dennis A. "Urban Planning as Policy Analysis: Management of
Urban Change." JOURNAL OF AMERICAN INSTITUTE OF PLANNERS 39
(January 1973): 13-22.

> The author reveals nine propositions which he feels characterize
> the activity of urban policy making, which he regards as first
> and foremost an inherently political activity. A list of skills
> and knowledge needed by professional policy analysts (planners)
> is then offered. One of the few articles providing such a wish
> list for the profession.

Tietz, Michael B. "Toward a Responsive Planning Methodology." In PLAN-
NING IN AMERICA: LEARNING FROM TURBULENCE, edited by David R.
Godschalk, pp. 86-110. Washington, D.C.: American Institute of Planners,
1974. 229 p.

> In a brilliant scholarly article about methods in planning, Tietz
> discusses the sociopolitical context within which planning methods
> have developed. He traces the history of methods in planning
> through four phases and offers a possible future direction for their
> development.

3.1.2 Decision Theory

Alexander, Christopher. NOTES ON THE SYNTHESIS OF FORM. Cambridge,
Mass.: Harvard University Press, 1964. 216 p.

> This is a classical work about problem solving and the development
> of systematic alternatives (decision theory). Though largely con-
> structed around problems of physical design, it can be viewed as
> a more general treatise on the subject. Included are a descrip-
> tion of the design problem, a vocabulary for problem solving, and
> a case study.

Bross, Irwin D. DESIGN FOR DECISION. New York: Macmillan, 1953.
276 p.

> An introduction to statistical decision theory and its application to
> managerial decision making. No mathematical background required.
> Used in many introductory planning methods courses.

Mack, Ruth P. PLANNING ON UNCERTAINTY: DECISION MAKING IN BUSINESS AND GOVERNMENT ADMINISTRATION. New York: Wiley-Interscience, 1971. xi, 233 p.

> An excellent summary of the decision-making literature which makes its own unique contributions. One of the "classics" for planners on this subject. Contains an interesting checklist of "ways to reduce uncertainty's cost."

Raiffa, Howard. DECISION ANALYSIS: INTRODUCTORY LECTURES ON CHOICES UNDER UNCERTAINTY. Reading, Mass.: Addison-Wesley, 1968. xxiii, 309 p.

> This is a classic work on statistical decision theory. Slightly beyond an introductory text, this is a compilation of lectures developed largely in a nonmathematical context. It is designed to introduce the subject of decision making to administrators and managers. The book is often used in planning methods courses.

Schlaifer, Robert. INTRODUCTION TO STATISTICS FOR BUSINESS DECISIONS. New York: McGraw-Hill, 1961. 382 p.

> This is a book that has been widely used in planning methods courses in the past for teaching probability, decision theory, and sampling. The author describes the book as a "unified treatment of classical and Bayesian statistics."

3.1.3 Systems Theory and Systems Analysis

Catanese, Anthony J[ames]., and Steiss, Alan W. SYSTEMIC PLANNING: THEORY AND APPLICATION. Lexington, Mass.: Lexington Books, 1970. xviii, 376 p.

> An effort to develop a theoretical structure forming a hybrid of systems analysis and comprehensive planning. The book contains several experimental case studies as well as evaluations of PPBS. It preceded much of the systems analysis literature of the 1970s.

de Neufville, Richard, and Stafford, Joseph. SYSTEMS ANALYSIS FOR ENGINEERS AND MANAGERS. New York: McGraw-Hill, 1971. xiii, 353 p.

> A text with examples of a number of systems analysis tools: optimization techniques, decision theory, causal modeling, and econometric methods. Good examples. Excellent references. Reasonable level of mathematical background is essential.

Drake, Alvin W., et al, eds. ANALYSIS OF PUBLIC SYSTEMS. Cambridge: MIT Press, 1972. x, 532 p.

> This book contains a collection of twenty-three articles largely focused on the use of quantitative, formal models as decision-making aids to problem solving in the public sector. The problems

addressed are largely noncomprehensive and smaller scale in nature and, as such, are categorized best as "operations research" as opposed to "planning" problems. A solid look at applications.

Friend, J[ohn].K., and Jessop, W.N. LOCAL GOVERNMENT AND STRATEGIC CHOICE: AN OPERATIONAL RESEARCH APPROACH TO THE PROCESS OF PUBLIC PLANNING. London: Tavistock Publications, 1969. xxvi, 296 p.

This book reports the results of four years of field work done by operations researchers in Coventry, England. After examining and describing the current state of the planning activity in Coventry, methods are suggested for improving the planning process. Included are a number of systems analysis techniques including cost-benefit, simulation, cost-effectiveness, decision theory, and sensitivity analysis.

Hughes, James [W.], and Mann, Lawrence. "Review Article: Systems and Planning Theory." JOURNAL OF AMERICAN INSTITUTE OF PLANNERS 35 (September 1969): 330-33.

In this article the authors review the relationship between general systems theory and some of the methods of systems analysis. They then review the relevance of both for the practice of urban planning. A concise review of the general systems theory literature for the uninitiated.

International City Management Association. APPLYING SYSTEMS ANALYSIS IN URBAN GOVERNMENT: THREE CASE STUDIES. Washington, D.C.: 1972. 77 p.

This report details the results of three demonstration projects on the use of systems analysis techniques at the local government level. It briefly describes the three cases: a fire station location, a housing inspection, and a community service center problem.

LaPatra, Jack W. APPLYING THE SYSTEMS APPROACH TO URBAN DEVELOPMENT. Stroudsburg, Pa.: Dowden, Hutchinson, and Ross, 1973. ix, 296 p.

This book supplies a smorgasbord of one- or two-page descriptions of largely operations research techniques and hints at their use in urban planning. Descriptions are rather superficial, and the tone of the book is such that the casual reader would be left with a disproportionate optimism for the tools and their use in an urban context.

McLoughlin, J. Brian. URBAN AND REGIONAL PLANNING: A SYSTEMS APPROACH. New York: Praeger, 1969. 331 p.

The author attempts with some success to develop a theoretical framework (systems theory) within which the techniques of physical planning can be understood. The book provides an approach--a conceptual scheme. Well written, but rather introductory and somewhat abstract in content.

Mesarovic, M.D., and Reisman, A., eds. SYSTEMS APPROACH AND THE CITY. New York: Elsevier, 1972. 481 p.

The book contains twenty papers presented at a symposium on "systems." It contains an unusual mixture of systems theory (theoretical systems concepts) and systems analysis (applications of the tools of operations research) papers, both oriented to "the city." A number of these papers are quite good, and not available elsewhere.

Quade, E.S., and Boucher, W.I. SYSTEMS ANALYSIS AND POLICY PLANNING: APPLICATIONS IN DEFENSE. New York: Elsevier, 1968. xxiii, 453 p.

Systems analysis according to the Rand Corporation, circa 1968. The procedure is laid out. Then a number of simplified case studies (from defense) are offered. Written for the intelligent layman.

Rosenbloom, Richard [S.], and Russell, John [R.]. NEW TOOLS FOR URBAN MANAGEMENT. Boston: Graduate School of Business Administration, Harvard University, 1971. xiii, 298 p.

The book reports on the results of a number of efforts to introduce the tools of systems analysis into the ongoing management of cities. Seven chapters compose the book, of which four are case studies. The thrust is the context for analysis, not the analysis itself. Other chapters address the issues surrounding the use of such analytic tools in an urban context.

Wheaton, William L.C. "Operations Research for Metropolitan Planning." JOURNAL OF AMERICAN INSTITUTE OF PLANNERS 29 (1963): 250-59.

In this methodologically optimistic paper, the author forecasts the involvement of the techniques of operations research in plan evaluation. He uses the Denver and Washington, D.C. plans as his case examples.

3.2 INFORMATION SOURCES AND PROCESSING

3.2.1 Data Sources and Indicators

Bauer, Raymond, ed. SOCIAL INDICATORS. Cambridge: MIT Press, 1966. xxi, 357 p.

This book helped initiate the "social indicators movement" in the

United States. The contributions of Bauer, Biderman, and Gross, after a decade of much additional work, remain insightful references to major conceptual issues in the social indicators field.

Felstead, William J., ed. QUALITATIVE METHODOLOGY. Chicago: Markham, 1970. 352 p.

This is an unusual book whose principal thrust is to question the value of highly complex quantitative methods in social science research and to present examples of nonquantitative techniques. It is a reader with thirty-one separate papers addressing the issues surrounding the use of qualitative methodologies (for example, participant observation).

Gross, Bertram M., ed. SOCIAL GOALS AND INDICATORS FOR AMERICAN SOCIETY. VOLUMES I AND II. Special Issues of THE ANNALS OF THE AMERICAN ACADEMY OF POLITICAL AND SOCIAL SCIENCE 371 and 373 (1967). 291 p., 313 p.

These two volumes contain a number of excellent articles on the development of social indicators. In addition to general methodological articles, specific substantive areas are treated, such as crime, health, and the arts.

Heer, David M., ed. SOCIAL STATISTICS AND THE CITY. Cambridge, Mass.: Joint Center for Urban Studies of the Massachusetts Institute of Technology and Harvard University, 1968. vii, 186 p.

This is a collection of six papers plus additional notes presented at a 1967 conference which focused on the difficulties the census had in 1960 of getting a full count of the urban poor and minorities. Good criticism of census procedures and a good introduction to many issues surrounding data collection by survey and census.

Holleb, Doris B. SOCIAL AND ECONOMIC INFORMATION FOR URBAN PLANNING. Vol. 1. Chicago: Center for Urban Studies, University of Chicago, 1969. 187 p.

This first volume attempts to delineate a field of urban planning activity and then describe its information needs and its general information sources. Its view of planning is at a somewhat introductory level. The thrust of the work is contained in the companion volume.

_____. SOCIAL AND ECONOMIC INFORMATION FOR URBAN PLANNING. Vol. 2. Chicago: Center for Urban Studies, University of Chicago, 1969. 312 p.

Contains the results of a 1967 survey of the social and economic statistics of potential use to urban planners. Not intended to be all inclusive, sources cited (particularly at the local level) are meant only to be suggestive. Directory is divided into ten subject categories, each further divided. One of the few directories of this kind.

International City Management Association. THE MUNICIPAL YEAR BOOK 1976. Washington, D.C.: 1922-- . Annual.

This yearbook reports statistics on a variety of topics of interest to urban managers and planners--statistics often derived from the ICMA yearly survey of local officials. It also contains articles analyzing the results of these surveys as well as other topics dealing with developments affecting local and state governments.

_____. URBAN DATA SERVICE REPORT. Vol. 8, no. 10. Washington, D.C.: October 1976.

Published monthly, "these reports are intended primarily to provide timely data in chart and tabular form, together with explanatory text, on current municipal government activities." Data usually came from ICMA surveys of local officials. This volume, as an example, was titled "Federal Grants Management: The City and County View."

Plessas, Demetrius J., and Fern, Recca. "Review Article: An Evaluation of Social Indicators." JOURNAL OF AMERICAN INSTITUTE OF PLANNERS 38 (January 1972): 43-51.

An excellent, comprehensive and critical review of the social indicators movement and its literature: theory, concepts, problems of operationalization, uses and misuses. Excellent list of references.

Sessions, Vivian S., ed. DIRECTORY OF DATA BASES IN THE SOCIAL AND BEHAVIORAL SCIENCES. New York: Sciences Associates International, 1974. xv, 300 p.

This volume is the result of an attempt to identify data bases (a file of collected information) in specific offices and libraries in the United States. Census materials and foreign materials are excluded. The results are "indicative," not comprehensive. In other words, one can get an idea of the types of data agencies collect but certainly cannot locate every U.S. data file in this volume.

U.S. Department of Commerce. Bureau of the Census. BUREAU OF THE CENSUS CATALOG: JANUARY-SEPTEMBER 1975. Washington, D.C.: Government Printing Office. Issued quarterly.

The catalog is designed to give users of Census Bureau data a means of locating it. Each quarterly issue gives descriptions of census materials released during that time period. A monthly supplementary report updates this quarterly volume.

Methods and Techniques

_____. COUNTY AND CITY DATA BOOK, 1972. Washington, D.C.: Government Printing Office, 1973. 1,020 p.

This book presents a wide variety of statistical information for counties, standard metropolitan statistical areas, cities, urbanized areas, and unincorporated places. It is tremendously valuable when the subject is intermetropolitan comparison.

_____. DIRECTORY OF FEDERAL STATISTICS FOR LOCAL AREAS: A GUIDE TO SOURCES, 1966. Washington, D.C.: Government Printing Office, 1966. vi, 156 p.

This manual is intended as a "comprehensive finding guide to current sources of federally published statistics for governmental and socioeconomic units below the state level. The units of analysis for which references are given include SMSAs, counties, and cities. The subject material is extraordinarily broad in scope.

_____. DIRECTORY OF NON-FEDERAL STATISTICS FOR STATES AND LOCAL AREAS. Washington, D.C.: Government Printing Office, 1969. vii, 678 p.

This volume serves as a reference to published sources of nonfederal statistics on social, political, and economic subjects. It is an index to about 1,800 statistical publications. The directory has two parts and an appendix. Part 1 is organized by states and outlying areas and covers thirteen major subjects. Part 2 is organized by these same subjects and reports for various units of analysis. The appendix provides additional secondary data source documents.

_____. STATISTICAL ABSTRACT OF THE UNITED STATES, 1974. Washington, D.C.: Government Printing Office, 1974. 1,028 p.

This is the annual standard summary of statistics on social, political, and economic aspects of the United States. It serves as a handy guide to other statistical publications and sources. The most common reporting unit is the country as a whole, but there are some state and regional data contained in the volume.

Warren, Roland. STUDYING YOUR COMMUNITY. New York: Free Press, 1955. 385 p.

This book, aimed at the layperson but helpful to the professional, is a how-to-study-the-community book. Warren defines the community very broadly, thus information is offered for study at a number of scales. Every aspect of community is considered: law enforcement, housing education, recreation, and so on. Its principal uses are suggested approach and data sources.

Webb, Eugene J., et al. UNOBTRUSIVE MEASURES: NONREACTIVE RESEARCH IN THE SOCIAL SCIENCES. Chicago: Rand-McNally, 1966. 225 p.

This is a classic book whose thrust is to offer alternatives to the traditional measurement devices of social scientists: survey research and secondary data sources developed from survey research. It also argues for a multiple-method approach to data gathering. Many of the suggested methods are unique.

Wilcox, Leslie D., et al. SOCIAL INDICATORS AND SOCIETAL MONITORING: AN ANNOTATED BIBLIOGRAPHY. San Francisco: Jossey-Bass/Elsevier, 1972. 480 p.

The most comprehensive literature search on social indicators available up to 1972. Over 1,000 separate listings, 600 of which are annotated. Annotated author, key-word, and address indexes are included. Though there are works cited that deal with urban social indicators that would pertain to planning at the local level, the thrust of the review is largely indicators in general (or at least national in scope) and is mostly oriented to the social sciences.

3.2.2 Information Systems

American Society of Planning Officials. THRESHOLD OF PLANNING INFORMATION SYSTEMS. Chicago: 1967. 108 p.

An early attempt to develop a framework and structure for the organization of large-scale information systems. The proposed system has limited use for the small planning office but may be usable, if dated, in larger offices.

Beshers, James, ed. COMPUTER METHODS IN THE ANALYSIS OF LARGE-SCALE SOCIAL SYSTEMS. 2d ed. Cambridge: MIT Press, 1968. 266 p.

This is a collection of papers occasioned by the first release, around 1965, of the Census Bureau's 1-1000 sample. The volume of data this sample provided was unprecedented. The authors addressed the numerous possibilities as well as problems that volume presented to social scientists. Data handling and model building were primary discussion items.

Branch, Melville [C.]. CITY PLANNING AND AERIAL INFORMATION. Cambridge, Mass.: Harvard University, 1971. 283 p.

This book deals with both the philosophy of the method and the "nuts-and-bolts" of application of aerial photography to urban planning. Based on a 1948 monograph, it is aimed at the practicing planner and is deliberately introductory in nature. It contains an excellent selected, annotated bibliography.

Duke, Richard D., ed. AUTOMATIC DATA PROCESSING: ITS APPLICATIONS TO URBAN PLANNING. East Lansing: Institute for Community Development and Services, Michigan State University, 1961. 112 p.

Methods and Techniques

An outdated technical report that has some usefulness as a historical piece which traces the movement towards greater quantifica-
tion and information handling by planners. The report is largely
related to Lansing area experiments.

Dunn, Edgar S., Jr. SOCIAL INFORMATION PROCESSING AND STATISTICAL
SYSTEMS--CHANGE AND REFORM. New York: Wiley, 1974. 256 p.

The book presents a theory of social information processing within
the context of the needs of the social and behavioral sciences
and the data provided at the national level. The author analyzes
current proposals for statistical reform and the essential elements
of data resources. An unusual, theoretical treatment of information and data processing.

Fite, Harry H. THE COMPUTER CHALLENGE TO URBAN PLANNERS AND
STATE ADMINISTRATORS. London: Macmillan and Co., 1965. 142 p.

A polemic in support of a greater use of computers and computer-
based analytic techniques in planning and state government. This
book is one of several generated during the heyday of efforts to
transfer systems techniques from aerospace industries to urban problems. Like the effort, this book is somewhat naive.

Hearle, Edward, and Mason, Raymond. A DATA PROCESSING SYSTEM FOR
STATE AND LOCAL GOVERNMENTS. Englewood Cliffs, N.J.: Prentice-
Hall, 1963. 176 p.

This book remains the classic on the application of information
systems technology to state and local governments. Though the
technical material obviously has become dated, the conceptual
foundation is sound. This was the basis for the development of
a number of urban information systems in the United States.

Hoos, Ida R. "Information Systems and Public Planning." MANAGEMENT
SCIENCE 13 (1967): 817-31.

The author begins by defining "information," "system," and "information system." She then takes apart the four following commonly
accepted beliefs: (1) more information makes for better plans and
decisions; (2) more and faster moving information would improve
government efficiency; (3) greater efficiency is always desirable;
(4) information system design is always best left to technical experts.

_____. "Systems Techniques for Managing Society: A Critique." PUBLIC
ADMINISTRATION REVIEW 33 (March-April 1973): 157-64.

The limitations of systems analysis are set out: its fiction of completeness, arbitrary boundary setting, predetermination by model
selection of variables and objectives, and obsession with data collection. Richly illustrated with examples.

McDowell, Bruce D., and Mindlin, Albert. "Planner's Notebook: Obtaining Metropolitan Planning Data from Local Governments." JOURNAL OF AMERICAN INSTITUTE OF PLANNERS 37 (March 1971): 111-15.

> This article describes an automated land use data system (at the individual parcel level) in use in the Washington, D.C. metropolitan area. Data problems are discussed, including specification of standard data items, land use coding, local data system development, and locational identification of land use parcels.

Sweeney, Stephen, and Charlesworth, James, eds. GOVERNING URBAN SOCIETY: NEW SCIENTIFIC APPROACHES. American Academy of Political and Science, Monograph 7. Philadelphia: 1967. 254 p.

> This document was published at the height of optimism over the injection of the new management science techniques and computer applications to the problems confronting urban governments. It is an interesting document read in that perspective, with a number of excellent papers.

Systems Development Corp. URBAN AND REGIONAL INFORMATION SYSTEMS. Washington, D.C.: Department of Housing and Urban Development, 1968. 331 p.

> Done for the Department of Housing and Urban Development, this book surveys the theory of urban information systems and presents numerous case studies. Since it was published early in the development of this field, the cases are embryonic, and there is little in the way of evaluation.

Webber, Melvin M. "The Roles of Intelligence Systems in Urban-Systems Planning." JOURNAL OF AMERICAN INSTITUTE OF PLANNERS 31 (November 1965): 289-96.

> In this classic article, Webber describes a new role for the planner--an information developer, processor, and provider. He describes "intelligence centers" where information on planning problems would be assembled and where various solutions could be generated. He saw the planner as "scientist-politician-planner" --all predicated on the planner's renewed strength when given new supplies of data and data processing equipment.

3.2.3 Survey Research Methods

Burton, T.L., and Cherry, G.E. SOCIAL RESEARCH TECHNIQUES FOR PLANNERS. London: Allen and Unwin, 1970. 137 p.

> The title is promising but the contents disappointing. This is largely a book about survey research methods. The technical chapters are weak in comparison with other books on survey research methods. The unique contribution the volume could pro-

vide would be a detailed discussion of the use of survey research
in planning. That is the objective of the first chapter, but it
falls short because it equates planning with the descriptive social
science literature.

Kish, Leslie. SURVEY SAMPLING. New York: Wiley, 1965. 635 p.

This is an excellent, if not _the_ excellent, book on sampling
methods. It is, in fact, a reference book. Straightforward though
it is, it shouldn't be approached without a grounding in statistical
tools. It is not a book for statisticians. For those planners en-
gaged in survey research, this is a fundamental volume for their
library. Excellent references.

Michigan, University of. Survey Research Center. INTERVIEWER'S MANUAL.
Ann Arbor: 1969. 95 p.

Produced by the most prestigious of the centers on survey research,
this document is an excellent introduction for those who will be
interviewing and a good reference work as well. Interviewing
principles and practice and sampling principles and procedures
are included.

Moser, C.A., and Kalton, G. SURVEY METHODS IN SOCIAL INVESTIGA-
TION. 2d ed. New York: Basic Books, 1972. 549 p.

An excellent, perhaps the best, introductory text on survey research methods. Covers all stages of the survey process including
analysis with emphasis on questions of sampling. An excellent
bibliography as well as good footnotes. Requires some statistical
knowledge, though the book could be considered nontechnical.

Oppenheim, A.N. QUESTIONNAIRE DESIGN AND ATTITUDE MEASURE-
MENT. New York: Basic Books, 1966. 298 p.

This is a basic reference book for planners involved in survey research. It is a "how-to" textbook for the development of a survey instrument--the questionnaire--question writing, attitude-
scaling, and projective techniques. It is an especially good
reference for scaling and attitude measurement techniques.

Saroff, Jerome R., and Levitan, Alberta Z., eds. SURVEY MANUAL FOR
COMPREHENSIVE URBAN PLANNING. Fairbanks: University of Alaska, Institute of Social, Economic, and Government Research, 1969. 143 p.

The authors developed this introductory manual for practicing
planners, around a survey project they ran in Providence, Rhode
Island. As such, it is very introductory and really sketches only
the highlights of the use of survey research methods in planning.
It is divided into two parts: the first fifty pages or so cover their

case study, its background and some results; following that, about seventy pages are devoted to an exposition of various aspects of the techniques used in survey sampling.

U.S. Department of Commerce. Bureau of the Census. SUPPLEMENTAL COURSES FOR CASE STUDIES IN SURVEYS AND CENSUSES: SAMPLING LECTURES. Washington, D.C.: Government Printing Office, 1968. ix, 85

A booklet of sampling lectures that provides a useful introduction to the topic.

Webb, Kenneth, and Hatry, Harry P. OBTAINING CITIZEN FEEDBACK: THE APPLICATION OF CITIZEN SURVEYS TO LOCAL GOVERNMENTS. Washington, D.C.: Urban Institute, 1973. 105 p.

Aimed at the layperson, this book takes a very pragmatic look at the use of survey research methods in local government. It answers a number of practical questions regarding the method. The appendix contains some examples of surveys used in local government: city services assessment, street cleaning evaluation, and recreation assessment, among others.

Weiss, Carol H., and Hatry, Harry P. AN INTRODUCTION TO SAMPLE SURVEYS FOR GOVERNMENT MANAGERS. Washington, D.C.: Urban Institute, 1971. 48 p.

This is an excellent introduction to survey research whose intended audience is the uninitiated government official or manager. Major issues surrounding the decision of whether or not to survey are considered, and cost estimates as they vary with the survey type are offered. A limited bibliography is included.

3.2.4 Descriptive Statistics

Blalock, Hubert M., Jr. SOCIAL STATISTICS. 2d ed. New York: McGraw-Hill, 1972. 583 p.

This text is widely used in planning methods courses. Written for those with only college algebra as preparation, it is considered an elementary text. However, it is not "cookbook" in approach but confronts and explains major theoretical points, important to understanding statistical thinking. Topics include descriptive, inductive, bivariate, and multivariate statistics, and sampling. Examples are primarily drawn from sociology.

Campbell, D.T., and Stanley, J.C. EXPERIMENTAL AND QUASIEXPERI-MENTAL DESIGNS FOR RESEARCH. Chicago: Rand-McNally, 1966. 84 p.

In this article, the authors examine sixteen experimental designs

against twelve possible problems in making valid inferences.
Despite its age, it remains an excellent reference book on research
methods in general and the design of experiments in particular.

Croxton, Frederick E., and Crowden, Dudley J. APPLIED GENERAL STATIS-
TICS. Englewood Cliffs, N.J.: Prentice-Hall, 1955. 944 p.

One of the most widely used statistics books for students in urban
planning. Deals somewhat with applications of statistics to a variety
of problems, but, of course, not necessarily planning-related ones.
Covers well the topics of nonlinear models not covered in other
statistical texts used in methods courses for planners.

Hodge, Gerald. "The Use and Mis-Use of Measurement Scales in City Planning." JOURNAL OF AMERICAN INSTITUTE OF PLANNERS 29 (1963): 112-
21.

In this article, the author criticizes a number of measurement
scales in use in planning (for example, a housing quality scale)
and lays out some of the dimensions of scaling techniques for the
profession.

Huff, Darrell. HOW TO LIE WITH STATISTICS. New York: Norton, 1954.
142 p.

This is an amusing little book filled with examples of the use and
misuse of descriptive statistics. Light reading, requiring little in
the way of statistical preparation.

Kendig, Hal. "Cluster Analysis to Classify Residential Areas: A Los Angeles
Application." JOURNAL OF AMERICAN INSTITUTE OF PLANNERS 42 (May
1976): 286-94.

The author reviews a number of techniques for summarizing statistics of subcity areas (for example, census tracts), including spatial
modeling, social area analysis, and factor analysis, and then
demonstrates the advantages for planners of cluster analysis. The
case study is Los Angeles, California.

Shevky, Eshrev, and Bell, Wendell. SOCIAL AREA ANALYSIS: THEORY,
ILLUSTRATIVE APPLICATION AND COMPUTATIONAL PROCEDURES. Stanford,
Calif.: Stanford University Press, 1955. 70 p.

This is a classic work in which the authors develop a theory of
urban structure and a measuring device (scaling technique) for
describing a case city (Los Angeles) and its subareas, in terms of
the model. A number of authors have built on this study, using
much more sophisticated statistical techniques and elaborate computational programs. It is basically a descriptive device.

Williams, Kenneth, ed. STATISTICS AND URBAN PLANNING. New York: Halsted Press, 1975. 189 p.

> Despite a promising title, this volume is a very superficial addition to the literature of planning methods. These are the proceedings of a 1972 international conference of urban statisticians. Two sections (eight chapters) deal with commutation and migration statistics. The other two sections, aimed at the book title directly, are disappointingly thin.

3.3 PROBLEM DEFINITION AND ANALYSIS

3.3.1 Population Analysis

Commission on Population Growth and the American Future. POPULATION AND THE AMERICAN FUTURE: THE REPORT OF THE COMMISSION ON POPULATION GROWTH AND THE AMERICAN FUTURE. Washington, D.C.: Government Printing Office, 1972. 7 vols. 186 p.

> This is the most current, most comprehensive, and most detailed report relating population variables to projected changes in American society. The titles of the volumes follow: (1) "Demographic and Social Aspects of Population Growth"; (2) "Economic Aspects of Population Change"; (3) "Population, Resources and the Environment"; (4) "Governance and Population"; (5) "Population Distribution and Policy"; (6) "Aspects of Population Growth Policy"; and (7) "Statements at Public Hearings of the Commission."

Gibbs, Jack P., ed. URBAN RESEARCH METHODS. Princeton, N.J.: Van Nostrand, 1961. 625 p.

> In a sense, the title is misleading. This is really a reader focusing on some, but certainly not all, of the methods used by human ecologists in their studies of urban areas. These are largely descriptive, not analytic methods. Some chapters, however, are of interest to planners, and there is an excellent bibliography.

Pittenger, Donald B. PROJECTING STATE AND LOCAL POPULATIONS. Cambridge, Mass.: Ballinger, 1976. 246 p.

> The book provides a clear presentation of population forecasting techniques for subnational areas. Though there is a historical review of forecasting techniques provided, the thrust of the book is a presentation of current methods.

Rogers, Andrei. INTRODUCTION TO MULTIREGIONAL MATHEMATICAL DEMOGRAPHY. New York: Wiley, 1975. 203 p.

> This book, the third in a series, develops a multiregional version of his previously developed single-region population projection model. In this model, interregional interactions are accounted for--

migration, as an example. It reviews this most recent development in demography. Advanced mathematically. Not an operational manual.

_____. MATRIX ANALYSIS OF INTERREGIONAL POPULATION GROWTH AND DISTRIBUTION. Berkeley and Los Angeles: University of California Press, 1968. 119 p.

The components of population change, birth, death, and migration are converted into a matrix model. This model is expanded from a single- to a three-region model. An understanding of matrix algebra, multiple regression, programming techniques, and probability theory is essential. A definitive work in this area.

U.S. Department of Commerce. Bureau of the Census. THE METHODS AND MATERIALS OF DEMOGRAPHY. 2 vols. Washington, D.C.: Government Printing Office, 1971. 888 p.

This is the single most comprehensive, up-to-date, and high-quality reference work on demographic methods. It is likely to stay the classic reference for some time. Methods relating to population size and distribution most relevant to planners are included. Good explanation of census techniques.

3.3.2 Systems Analysis Tools

Baumol, William. ECONOMIC THEORY AND OPERATIONS ANALYSIS. 2d ed. Englewood Cliffs, N.J.: Prentice-Hall, 1965. 606 p.

This is a book about the tools of microeconomic analysis and mathematical economics, linear and nonlinear programming, and input-output analysis, among many others. It is a book about difficult concepts that is exemplary for its clarity and relative ease of reading.

Bellman, Richard E., and Dreyfus, Stuart E. APPLIED DYNAMIC PROGRAMMING. Princeton, N.J.: Princeton University Press, 1962. 363 p.

This is the classic work on the topic done by its originators. The book attempts to display applications within a managerial decision-making context.

Carr, Charles R., and Howe, Charles W. QUANTITATIVE DECISION PROCEDURES IN MANAGEMENT AND ECONOMICS: DETERMINISTIC THEORY AND APPLICATIONS. New York: McGraw-Hill, 1964. 383 p.

This book is one of the best available on the topic of deterministic theory and its application in both simple and complex optimization models. Clear in its presentation of theory, it also presents examples of application to management problems. It is suggestive of possible application in urban analysis.

Dantzig, George G. LINEAR PROGRAMMING AND EXTENSIONS. Princeton, N.J.: Princeton University Press, 1963. 632 p.

>   This book is written by a leader in the field of linear programming. It is difficult, both theoretically and mathematically, and is intended for more advanced students of the topic.

Draper, Norman, and Smith, Harry. APPLIED REGRESSION ANALYSIS. New York: Wiley, 1966. 407 p.

>   This textbook is a basic advanced reference on the topic of regression analysis. Very detailed and broad in scope, it assumes the reader has a working knowledge of many statistical techniques.

Hadley, G. NON-LINEAR AND DYNAMIC PROGRAMMING. Reading, Mass.: Addison-Wesley, 1964. 484 p.

>   This book is the classical work on the topic. As such, it is both a basic reference and a highly mathematical and technical treatment.

Hanssmann, Fred. OPERATIONS RESEARCH TECHNIQUES FOR CAPITAL INVESTMENT. New York: Wiley, 1968. 269 p.

>   The book inventories the potential contributions of operations research to the solution of investment problems. Chapter 1 is a condensed review of operations research methodology. The remaining chapters deal with the application of the tools to investment decisions, including some interesting case studies.

Johnston, John. ECONOMETRIC METHODS. New York: McGraw-Hill, 1963. 300 p.

>   This book is aimed at those who have a thorough grounding in statistical theory and method and is a self-contained exposition of econometric methods. The book is divided into two parts. Part 1 provides a complete description of the linear normal regression model. Part 2 examines the main statistical methods used to estimate econometric models.

Lazarsfeld, Paul F., ed. MATHEMATICAL THINKING IN THE SOCIAL SCIENCES. Glencoe, Ill.: Free Press, 1954. 444 p.

>   This book was one of the first to try to apply the concepts of probability theory to a number of social science problems. As such, many of the topics in it are of interest to urban planners.

Levin, Richard I., and Lamone, Rudolph P. LINEAR PROGRAMMING FOR MANAGEMENT DECISION. Homewood, Ill.: Richard D. Irwin, 1969. 308 p.

>   This is an introductory textbook on the topic, presumably written

for nonmathematicians. The concepts of linear programming are
presented in an applied framework of management decision making.
A section is included on canned linear programming computer
programs.

Lipschutz, Seymour. THEORY AND PROBLEMS OF FINITE MATHEMATICS.
New York: Schaum, 1966. 156 p.

This book is part of a college outline series. As such, it deals
with matrix methods in a very easily understood way. There are
problems given with answers so that the student can check his or
her own work.

Perlis, Sam. THEORY OF MATRICES. Reading, Mass.: Addison-Wesley,
1952. 237 p.

The advantage of this book on matrix methods is that it is beyond
most textbooks in scope and detail. However, it is well written
and, with work, is accessible to a fairly wide audience.

Robson, B.T. URBAN ANALYSIS. New York: Cambridge University Press,
1969. 294 p.

The title is deceiving, in a sense, because one expects more than
is here. This is largely a book on the use of multivariate statistical techniques on intraurban sociological data. Largely descriptive social science, but an excellent presentation of such.

Rogers, Andrei. MATRIX METHODS IN URBAN AND REGIONAL ANALYSIS.
San Francisco: Holden-Day, 1971. 499 p.

A comprehensive review of matrix-oriented quantitative analysis
methods: matrix operations, input-output, computer programming,
statistical analysis, linear programming, game theory, network
analysis, work programming. Important are the excellent examples
of application of these tools to urban-regional planning situations.

Scientific American. MATHEMATICAL THINKING IN THE BEHAVIORAL SCI-
ENCES: READINGS FROM SCIENTIFIC AMERICAN. San Francisco: W.H.
Freeman, 1968. 231 p.

This is a collection of articles dating from 1948 to 1968 on the
subject of the use of mathematical thinking for problem-solving
in the social and behavioral sciences. A number of excellent
introductory papers, for example, on the topic of probability
theory. Very introductory in nature.

Taylor, Angus E. CALCULUS WITH ANALYTIC GEOMETRY. Englewood
Cliffs, N.J.: Prentice-Hall, 1959. 617 p.

This is a classic calculus textbook. As such, it serves as a reference source on the topic. The inclusion of analytic geometry makes it even more relevant to planners, since it applies to many problems with a spatial focus.

Tocher, K.D. THE ART OF SIMULATION. Princeton, N.J.: Van Nostrand, 1963. 184 p.

Using general systems theory as a base, this book presents both the theory and method of simulation. It is a classic work on the topic.

Wagner, Harvey M. PRINCIPLES OF OPERATIONS RESEARCH. Englewood Cliffs, N.J.: Prentice-Hall, 1969. v, 937 p.

This is a general introduction to operations research and a specific treatment of nonlinear, dynamic and stochastic programming. It is intermediate in its demand for a mathematical background. It presents the tools in the context of management problem solving.

Wonnacott, Ronald, and Wonnacott, Thomas. ECONOMETRICS. New York: Wiley, 1970. 445 p.

This book offers an excellent treatment of econometric methods. It is divided into two parts: an elementary section for those with only a very basic statistics background, and an advanced section for those with background in calculus and matrix algebra. The topics are paralleled in both sections with part 2 being heavily mathematical. Part 1 serves as an excellent introduction to the topic.

3.3.3 Simulation, Modeling, and Gaming: General

Abt, Clark C. SERIOUS GAMES. New York: Viking, 1970. 176 p.

Authored by the leader of a major gaming consulting firm, this book discusses a number of political, military, and business games --with many of the examples drawn from the firm's own work.

Alonso, William. "Predicting Best with Imperfect Data." JOURNAL OF AMERICAN INSTITUTE OF PLANNERS 34 (July 1968): 248-55.

In this article, Alonso attacks the quite technical problem of the cumulation of error in urban models. He demonstrates his reservations statistically and makes suggestions about the structure of future models. At the same time, however, he comments on the general state of modeling within the profession, and the need for more evaluation of their effectiveness.

American Society of Planning Officials. ANALYTICAL TECHNIQUES. Papers presented at the 1970 ASPO National Planning Conference. Chicago: 1970. 89 p.

Methods and Techniques

A series of presentations on the philosophical and practical issues surrounding the use of analytical techniques (especially models). The presentations were an uneven lot, and the papers represent much overlap and generality.

Brewer, Garry D. POLITICIANS, BUREAUCRATS AND THE CONSULTANT: A CRITIQUE OF URBAN PROBLEM SOLVING. New York: Basic Books, 1973. 291 p.

This is a unique volume. Its concern is the use and misuse of computer models in policy-making contexts. The author studies the social settings, the actors, and the models themselves. Two specific contexts are studied: the San Francisco and Pittsburgh community renewal programs.

Brown, H. James, et al. EMPIRICAL MODELS OF URBAN LAND USE: SUGGESTIONS ON RESEARCH OBJECTIVES AND ORGANIZATION. New York: National Bureau of Economic Research, 1972. 100 p.

This is a basic book on land use and transportation models. Five major transportation studies completed in the United States are examined: Puget Sound, southeastern Wisconsin, Atlanta, Detroit, and San Francisco. An overview of both institutional context and methodologies is given, as well as a critique of the current state-of-the-art. Key references to all of the five studies are listed.

Creighton, Roger L. URBAN TRANSPORTATION PLANNING. Urbana: University of Illinois Press, 1970. 376 p.

This text gathers together much of the previously scattered material relevant to transportation planning. The focus is an overall transportation planning methodology and its implications for the larger context--the planning of metropolitan regions.

Duke, Richard D. GAMING: THE FUTURE'S LANGUAGE. New York: Halsted Press, 1974. 223 p.

Richard Duke is recognized as the foremost leader of the urban-gaming field. This book brings together his thoughts on gaming for the first time. It is an attempt to develop a "unifying perspective on the nature of gaming." Duke sees games as a form of communication, and that theoretical formulation is used to discuss game design and, finally, the future of gaming. A seminal work in the field.

Feldt, Allan G. "Operational Gaming in Planning Education." JOURNAL OF AMERICAN INSTITUTE OF PLANNERS 32 (January 1966): 17-23.

This is one of the early papers of Allan Feldt, the designer of the COMMUNITY LAND USE GAME (see p. 104). He describes

the game in general terms and discusses the playing experiences
with it. The thrust of this article is the use of games as teaching and
and communication devices as opposed to simulations.

Greenblat, Cathy S., and Duke, Richard D. GAMING-SIMULATION: RA-
TIONALE, DESIGN AND APPLICATIONS. New York: Halsted Press, 1975.
435 p.

Contained in this book are "overview essays" by the authors on
three topics: the rationale for gaming, game design, and applications. These essays are supplemented by a set of articles by other
authors that either give depth to a specific topic, expand upon
an essay idea, or offer examples of points made in the essays. A
key work in the previously dispersed gaming literature.

Harris, Britton. "Planning Method: The State of the Art." In PLANNING IN
AMERICA: LEARNING FROM TURBULENCE, edited by David R. Godschalk,
pp. 62-85. Washington, D.C.: American Institute of Planners, 1974. 229 p.

In this article, Harris defines methodology in planning (or at least
the methodology he will deal with) as synonymous with modeling.
He then provides an excellent review of the state of that particular method in 1974. Harris views these methods as the ones of
importance because: "unlike a number of informal and sometimes
archaic planning methods, the methods I will discuss are capable
of systematic evaluation, transmission, and improvement."

_____. "Plan or Projection: An Examination of the Use of Models in Plan-
ning." JOURNAL OF AMERICAN INSTITUTE OF PLANNERS 26 (December
1960): 265-72.

By now the discussion of the use of models in planning had become
heated. In this article, Harris attempted to describe the difference
between planning and projection, and argues for a more scientific
base for planning practice.

_____. "Quantitative Models of Urban Development: Their Role in Metro-
politan Policy-Making." In ISSUES IN URBAN ECONOMICS, edited by Harvey
S. Perloff and Lowdon Wingo, Jr., pp. 363-412. Baltimore, Md.: Johns
Hopkins Press, 1968. 668 p.

In this article, the leading spokesman for the development and use
of models in planning first reviews some "dimensions along which
models may be classified." He then discusses the applications of
these dimensions in a "problems" context. This is a normative
paper in many respects, for the politics of the use of modeling in
planning is not discussed. An excellent review paper.

_____, ed. "Urban Development Models: New Tools for Planning." A
special issue of the JOURNAL OF AMERICAN INSTITUTE OF PLANNERS 31
(May 1965): entire issue.

This was an extremely important issue of the journal. It was more than just an issue devoted to modeling. It marked the transition in the theory and practice of planning to another stage--a point at which the new wave of social science began to flood the profession. Included are many classic articles on models and planning as well as reviews of many important books about urban and regional theory and modeling.

Hemmins, George, ed. URBAN DEVELOPMENT MODELS, Special Report 97. Washington, D.C.: Highway Research Board, National Research Council, 1968. 266 p.

This volume reports the results of a Conference on Urban Development Models held at Dartmouth College in 1967. It was a state-of-the-art conference and as such assessed the relationship of modeling activity to planning-agency activity in general.

Kilbridge, Maurice, et al. URBAN ANALYSIS. Boston: Graduate School of Business Administration, Harvard University, 1970. 332 p.

The book offers several important contributions. First, it offers several typologies of models and attempts to categorize each major U.S. modeling effort by type. Second, there is an extensive bibliography, also typologized and well indexed. The chapters on technical steps of model development are less central.

Lee, Douglas B., Jr. "Requiem for Large Scale Models." JOURNAL OF AMERICAN INSTITUTE OF PLANNERS 39 (May 1973): 163-78.

This is a classical article, a watershed on the topography of the planning profession. Lee is very critical of the direction of the modeling movement (large-scale, comprehensive models). He suggests a new direction: small-scale, policy-oriented, problem-directed modeling efforts. Little criticism or evaluation at all of this major activity had been published before this article.

Meier, Richard L., and Duke, Richard D. "Gaming Simulation for Urban Planning." JOURNAL OF AMERICAN INSTITUTE OF PLANNERS 32 (January 1966): 3-17.

This was an article written as Duke was about to introduce his first complex game called Metropolis. This is a very early gaming article oriented specifically to gaming in urban planning. It is, of course, optimistic and expansionist in its tone. There are a number of "if, then" statements concerning the types of situations in planning amenable to the development of simulation-game models, pure simulations, and, lastly, pure games.

Pack, Janet Rothenberg. "The Use of Urban Models: Report on a Survey of Planning Organizations." JOURNAL OF AMERICAN INSTITUTE OF PLANNERS 41 (May 1975): 191-99.

In this survey of nearly 1,500 planning agencies, the author describes the use of models on the part of such agencies, examining types of models versus types of agencies along with agency attitudes toward their use. A unique study of the use of models at this time. There was a previous survey by George Hemmens reported in Hemmens (1968) 3.3.3, p. 102.

Reif, Benjamin. MODELS IN URBAN AND REGIONAL PLANNING. London: Leonard Hill Books, 1973. 246 p.

This book places urban spatial models in the context of both the systems approach and the planning process, and discusses the conceptual framework and mathematics of model building. It presents abbreviated descriptions of a number of models in use and then an appraisal of the status of urban spatial modeling in general. A good (modeling) glossary of terms is included.

Sweet, David C., ed. MODELS OF URBAN STRUCTURE. Lexington, Mass.: Lexington Books, 1972. 252 p.

Presents several examples of urban development models. Analyzes the use of models in a planning context. Speculates on their use in the 1970s. Good annotated bibliography of specific models. Reports the results of an independent survey of 226 planning agencies on their use of models.

Voorhees, Alan M., ed. "Land Use and Traffic Models: A Progress Report." A special issue of the JOURNAL OF AMERICAN INSTITUTE OF PLANNERS 25 (May 1959): entire issue.

This was the first issue of the journal devoted entirely to urban land use and traffic models. It is introduced by journal editor Mel Webber, in the most optimistic of tones, as a new line of research and discovery in planning. The models are largely descriptive in nature. A number of classic articles appear in this seminal edition of the journal. Excellent bibliography as of this date.

Wilson, A.G. URBAN AND REGIONAL MODELS IN GEOGRAPHY AND PLANNING. New York: Wiley, 1975. 418 p.

The principal thrust of this volume is the mathematical display of a number of spatial models (267 pages). Its discussion of the use of models in planning is dated, and weak at best. But its mathematical presentation is excellent, and understandable. Mathematical background is essential.

3.3.4 Simulation, Modeling, and Gaming: Examples

Cesario, Frank J. "A Primer on Entropy Modeling." JOURNAL OF AMERICAN INSTITUTE OF PLANNERS 41 (1975): 40-48.

Methods and Techniques

This article explains the statistical concept of entropy and its recently discovered relevance to modeling urban and regional phenomena. Simple examples of the concept are presented.

Feldt, Allan G., et al. CLUG: THE COMMUNITY LAND USE GAME. PLAYER'S MANUAL WITH SELECTED READINGS. New York: Free Press, 1972. 206 p.

The CLUG game has become the classic systemic land use game, a game analogy to Lowry's model. The book presents a general discussion of gaming, the rules of play, and, finally, some readings and experiments that can be played with the game. For example, there is an experiment that replaces the property tax in the game with a land tax. Paper game components are included in the book.

Forrester, Jay [W.]. "A Deeper Knowledge of Social Systems." TECHNOLOGY REVIEW 71 (1969): 22-31.

Probably the most accessible and condensed version of the Forrester modeling approach. Presentation of concepts and examples of their use in his model of "urban dynamics."

_____. URBAN DYNAMICS. Cambridge: MIT Press, 1969. xiii, 285 p.

This work, when introduced, caused great furor. By now most have come to regard its real policy output as worthless--that is, the results of the modeling itself were misleading. There is not agreement, however, on the usefulness of the modeling approach itself. The book itself is readable and is a distinctive modeling approach.

Goldner, William. "The Lowry Model Heritage." JOURNAL OF AMERICAN INSTITUTE OF PLANNERS 37 (March 1971): 100-10.

A brief review of the Lowry model itself is first developed. Then the author reviews a number of the derivative models including TOMM, BASS, Garin-Rogers, CLUG, PLUM, and so forth.

Lowry, Ira. A MODEL OF METROPOLIS. Santa Monica, Calif.: RAND Corp., 1964. xi, 136 p.

Lowry developed his model working with the Pittsburgh Regional Planning Association. The model itself is the archetype urban market simulation model, involving the allocation of industrial, residential, and service sectors. The model has been replicated in many other instances. See Goldner (1971) above, this section.

Schlager, Kenneth J. "A Land Use Plan Design Model." JOURNAL OF AMERICAN INSTITUTE OF PLANNERS 31 (May 1965): 103-10.

One of the few demonstrations of optimization techniques (linear and nonlinear programming) in planning. The techniques are considered more important pedagogically than operationally.

Wilson, A.G. ENTROPY IN URBAN AND REGIONAL MODELING. London: Pion, 1970. 166 p.

Entropy is a theory, as explained by Wilson, that can be seen to underlie a number of planning interests: trip distribution, modal split, route split, interregional commodity flows, and locational decisions. The book contains 474 equations, is rather murky, and definitely is not for the faint of mathematical heart.

3.3.5 Forecasting Techniques

Delbecq, Andre L., et al. GROUP TECHNIQUES FOR PROGRAM PLANNING. A GUIDE TO NOMINAL GROUP AND DELPHI PROCESSES. Glenview, Ill.: Scott, Foresman, 1975.

This book is a basic manual of instruction in how to conduct both nominal group (chapter 3) and Delphi (chapter 4) sessions. Additionally, the entire range of small group decision making is explored along with the relevance of these techniques to these decisions, which include citizen participation and exploratory research.

Fowles, Gib. "An Overview of Social Forecasting Procedures." JOURNAL OF AMERICAN INSTITUTE OF PLANNERS 42 (1976): 253-63.

A state-of-the-art article about futures research which describes all the methods in use for social forecasting and projects to a future futures methodology. Good bibliography.

Martino, Joseph. TECHNOLOGICAL FORECASTING FOR DECISIONMAKING. New York: Elsevier, 1972. 768 p.

The book is a comprehensive advanced treatment of the broad topic of technological forecasting. It is divided into three parts: (1) a discussion of forecasting methods, (2) a description of the applications of forecasting to decision making, and (3) a guide to preparing actual forecasts in a number of contexts. As of this writing, this is the most important source book on this topic.

OECD Working Symposium on Long-Range Forecasting and Planning. PERSPECTIVES OF PLANNING. PROCEEDINGS OF THE ORGANIZATION FOR ECONOMIC COOPERATION AND DEVELOPMENT, (OECD). WORKING SYMPOSIUM ON LONG RANGE FORECASTING AND PLANNING. Paris: 1968. 527 p.

The predictive and projective part of the planning process is covered here in a very comprehensive survey of approaches and methods. Of special value for its descriptions of nontraditional and nonquantitative techniques, such as the Delphi method, the Morphological Box, and so forth.

_____. TECHNOLOGICAL PLANNING AND SOCIAL FUTURES. New York: Wiley, 1972. 256 p.

This book is made up of articles published by the author since his first survey of forecasting methods (Paris: OECD, 1967). It is loosely organized, with sections and chapters centered on the following topics: a general framework for long-range thinking, a survey of methodologies, organizational ramifications, roles and responsibilities, world systems, and future applications.

Sackman, Harold. DELPHI CRITIQUE. Lexington, Mass.: Lexington Books, D.C. Heath, 1975. 145 p.

Delphi is a method which attempts to elicit expert opinion in a systematic manner. This book provides a scientific appraisal of Delphi from a number of points of view--assumption, principles, methodology, against scientific standards, and so forth. Recommendations are made for its future use. Half the book is a "semiannotated" bibliography on Delphi.

3.3.6 Regional Science and Location Theory

Alonso, William. LOCATION AND LAND USE: TOWARDS A GENERAL THEORY OF LAND RENT. Cambridge, Mass.: Harvard University Press, 1964. 204 p.

The product of Alonso's doctoral dissertation, this monograph offers a highly mathematical look at the economics of location within a city. It is a general formulation of the "classic theory of rent and location." This is a classic work in location theory, inaccessible to those without an elementary background in both mathematics and economics.

Bendavid, Avrom. REGIONAL ECONOMIC ANALYSIS FOR PRACTITIONERS: AN INTRODUCTION TO COMMON DESCRIPTIVE METHODS. Rev. ed. New York: Praeger, 1974. 220 p.

This is a book written, unapologetically, for practitioners in the field of regional economic planning. It assumes a relatively low level of research infrastructure (data, computers, manpower, etc.) that one might encounter in a developing country. Nonmathematical in nature, it covers the principal methodologies of regional economic analysis. A bibliography on more advanced work is included.

Berry, Brian J.L., and Horton, Frank E. GEOGRAPHIC PERSPECTIVES ON URBAN SYSTEMS. Englewood Cliffs, N.J.: Prentice-Hall, 1970. xii, 564 p.

This is a relatively comprehensive volume which defines the field of urban geography through both text and readings. The book presents a theory of urban geography. But, in addition, it reviews a number of methodologies used by urban geographers and urban planners.

Czamanski, Stan. REGIONAL SCIENCE TECHNIQUES IN PRACTICE. Lexington, Mass.: Lexington Books, D.C. Heath, 1972. 457 p.

The author skillfully applies techniques of economic accounting, input-output analysis, econometrics, and other related techniques to the regional economy of Nova Scotia, Canada. While basic understanding of the techniques is assumed, data sources, competing measurement approaches, and policy context are assessed in reporting the applications. Chapters usually end with a specific discussion of the results which have policy relevance.

Gibson, W.L., Jr., et al. METHODS FOR LAND ECONOMICS RESEARCH. Lincoln: University of Nebraska, 1966. 242 p.

This book is the result of a 1965 conference on land economics research methodology held at Virginia Polytechnic Institute. It is divided into three sections: a history of method in land economics (one paper), the philosophy of inquiry (four papers), and the empirical techniques of analysis (seven papers). The skills section is unique in that it specifies the types of problems that quantitative techniques address, as well as characteristics of the technique.

Hickman, Bert G., ed. QUANTITATIVE PLANNING OF ECONOMIC POLICY. Conference papers of the Social Science Research Council Committee on Economic Stability. Washington, D.C.: Brookings Institution, 1965. 269 p.

The thrust of this book is an investigation of the usefulness of quantitative methods as they are used in national macroeconomic policy making. The audience is intended to be policymakers, so it is highly readable. Two types of papers are included: reviews of theory and technique of quantitative analysis, and case studies of the use of techniques in the Netherlands, Japan, and France.

Hirsch, Werner Z. URBAN ECONOMIC ANALYSIS. New York: McGraw-Hill, 1973. 450 p.

This is an excellent textbook. It combines a theoretical approach to urban economics which includes both micro- and macro-analytic models. In addition, it discusses a number of urban economic "issues" and presents a number of the tools of urban economic analysis.

_____, ed. ELEMENTS OF REGIONAL ACCOUNTS. Baltimore, Md.: Johns Hopkins Press, 1964. xviii, 221 p.

This book contains nine papers (with comments on them) presented at the Second Conference on Regional Accounts held in 1962 by

Resources for the Future. The thrust of the papers is the "provision of information for decision makers at the regional level." However the papers are somewhat abstract in nature, calling for more data than was (is) currently available. Solid theoretical work lacking immediate examples of application. Economics background needed to read some of the papers.

Hochwald, Werner, ed. DESIGN OF REGIONAL ACCOUNTS, PAPERS. Baltimore, Md.: Johns Hopkins Press for Resources for the Future, 1961. 281 p.

A collection of nine papers delivered at a 1960 conference of the Committee of Regional Accounts of Resources for the Future. (This is the first of three volumes put out by RFF.) To some degree an uneven collection, with some papers really not addressing the topic. Discusses the differences between national and regional accounts, data, and implementation problems.

Hoover, Edgar M. AN INTRODUCTION TO REGIONAL ECONOMICS. 2d ed. New York: Knopf, 1975. 395 p.

The first edition of this book was published in 1971. It is primarily intended as a text for introductory courses in regional economics. Minimal mathematics and economics background is assumed. The author eschews the use of current topics, concentrating instead on a clear, concise examination of more general theories. The book is not intended as a "how-to" book on locational decisions. Probably the best introduction to the topic available at this time.

_____. THE LOCATION OF ECONOMIC ACTIVITY. New York: McGraw-Hill, 1948. 310 p.

This book is a classic on the subject of location theory. Eighteen chapters are divided into four sections: locational preferences and patterns, locational change and adjustment, the locational significance of boundaries, and locational objectives and public policy.

Hoyt, Homer. THE STRUCTURE AND GROWTH OF RESIDENTIAL NEIGHBORHOODS IN AMERICAN CITIES. Washington, D.C.: Superintendent of Documents, 1939. 178 p.

This is the classic study of the location of activities within urban areas. It is quite empirical, drawing on housing and population statistics that were available to this extent and magnitude for the first time in the United States. Generously illustrated with maps of the patterns of population and housing variables in a number of case cities, circa 1935.

Isard, Walter. INTRODUCTION TO REGIONAL SCIENCE. Englewood Cliffs, N.J.: Prentice-Hall, 1975. 506 p.

This is the first attempt to produce a textbook at an introductory level on the subject of regional science--this one done by the father of the field, Walter Isard. Like the field, the book is eclectic--perhaps to a fault. This should be considered a standard classic--a seminal work. But though it is too early to say, it seems unlikely that it will become so because of its diffuse nature.

_____. LOCATION AND SPACE-ECONOMY; A GENERAL THEORY RELATING TO INDUSTRIAL LOCATION, MARKET AREAS, LAND USE, TRADE, AND URBAN STRUCTURE. Cambridge and New York: MIT Press and Wiley, 1956. 350 p.

In this seminal work, Isard attempted to develop a general theory of location and space and, therefore, urban and regional development over time and space. The book contains eleven chapters that deal with a review of general theories, transport, location of the firm, agglomeration analysis, trade theory, and a mathematical formulation of general location theory, among others.

Isard, Walter, et al. METHODS OF REGIONAL ANALYSIS. New York: MIT Press and Wiley, 1960. 784 p.

A seminal work in regional science. State-of-the-art as well as a definition of the discipline, circa 1960. The book is very broad in scope, and nothing of this scope has since appeared. Many of the specific topics are, by now, better covered by other dispersed sources, however.

Kain, John [F.], ed. ESSAYS ON URBAN SPATIAL STRUCTURE. Cambridge, Mass.: Ballinger, 1975. 412 p.

This is a collection of seventeen essays introduced by the editor with a concise history and projection for further development of the field of urban economics. It is really state-of-the-art thinking on a number of critical urban economic issues, including residential and commuting choice, job location, social discrimination, housing markets, and transportation. For the most part, it is quite readable for those with a minimum of quantitative training.

Kain, John F., and Meyer, John R., eds. ESSAYS IN REGIONAL ECONOMICS. Cambridge, Mass.: Harvard University Press, 1971. 422 p.

Twelve papers survey various aspects of regional economic development. An introductory essay by the editors places these papers in the context of the state-of-the-field of regional economics. Broad topics covered include the objectives of regional development policy, the impact of industrial development, regional growth and capital flows, southern development, and regional models. For the most part, it is quite readable for those with a minimum of quantitative training.

Miernyk, William. THE ELEMENTS OF INPUT-OUTPUT ANALYSIS. New York: Random House, 1965.

This is a standard introductory reference to input-output analysis, written by one of the most prominent scholars of regional input-output studies. The book covers the accounting and basic analytical uses of input-output. The discussion of more advanced applications in later chapters is excellent but somewhat dated. Several tear-out tables and numerical examples make the book fine for classroom use.

Page, Alfred, and Seyfried, Warren, eds. URBAN ANALYSIS: READINGS IN HOUSING AND URBAN DEVELOPMENT. Glenview, Ill.: Scott, Foresman, 1970. 427 p.

The short title of this volume is a deceptive title. In fact, this is a collection of essays, largely by economists, addressing a variety of topics connected to housing markets and housing location. Thirty-five papers are contained in the volume, many of them classics.

Richardson, Harry W. INPUT-OUTPUT AND REGIONAL ECONOMICS. New York: Halsted, 1973. 306 p.

The author has compiled a well-organized survey of regional input-output studies emphasizing the conceptual, methodological, and analytical aspects of the tool. The attempt at comprehensive coverage of the regional Anglo-American literature leads to superficial treatment of several advanced topics (such as multiregional input-output). Overall, the book is a very useful survey reference.

3.4 EVALUATION AND IMPLEMENTATION

3.4.1 Evaluation: General

Boyce, David E.; Day, Norman D.; and McDonald, Chris. METROPOLITAN PLAN MAKING: AN ANALYSIS OF EXPERIENCE WITH THE PREPARATION AND EVALUATION OF ALTERNATIVE LAND USE AND TRANSPORTATION PLANS. Monograph Series No. 4. Philadelphia: Regional Science Research Institute, 1970. 475 p. Paperbound.

The classic study documenting seven major land use and transportation studies done prior to 1967: Baltimore, Boston, Chicago, Milwaukee, Minneapolis-St. Paul, New York, Philadelphia. Develops generalized descriptions of the planning process including the plan evaluation stage. Makes recommendations for changes in the planning process.

Cochrane, Robert A., and Wamble, Joseph E. "Technical Report: Discounted Cash Flow Analysis and Plan Evaluation." JOURNAL OF AMERICAN INSTITUTE OF PLANNERS 37 (September 1971): 338-43.

In this article, discounted cash-flow analysis is used to evaluate a specific development project: Port Moresby, the capital city of the Territory of Papua and New Guinea. Implications for the use of this technique in other contexts are examined.

Hill, Morris. "A Goals-Achievement Matrix for Evaluating Alternative Plans." JOURNAL OF AMERICAN INSTITUTE OF PLANNERS 34 (January 1968): 19-29.

A summary of the development of Hill's goals-achievement matrix developed in his doctoral work.

_____. PLANNING FOR MULTIPLE OBJECTIVES: AN APPROACH TO THE EVALUATION OF TRANSPORTATION PLANS. Philadelphia: Regional Science Research Institute, 1973. 273 p.

The book evaluates cost-benefit analysis as an approach to decision making on water resource, highway, and urban development problems. Hill presents his goals-achievement matrix technique as an alternative method of plan evaluation. The method is then demonstrated by application to the evaluation of alternative transportation plans through theory, and then a case study.

Hudson, Barclay M., et al. "Local Impact Evaluation in the Design of Large-Scale Urban Systems." JOURNAL OF AMERICAN INSTITUTE OF PLANNERS 40 (July 1974): 255-65.

The conflict between a large systems "public interest" and the diverse interests of small communities affected by large public projects is explored vis-à-vis a number of evaluative procedures and each of their abilities to cope with conflict: benefit-cost, social benefit-cost, cost-effectiveness, computer interaction, and a new technique called "dialactical scanning."

Kozlowski, J., and Hughes, J.T. THRESHOLD ANALYSIS: A QUANTITATIVE PLANNING METHOD. London: Architectural Press, 1972. 286 p.

The author introduced this technique in the mid-sixties in the United Kingdom. Its main use is in narrowing the range of possibilities for physical development by analyzing those characteristics of sites that would cause a discontinuity in the marginal cost curve of the project. Topography and inefficient use of utilities are examples of probable causes.

Lichfield, Nathaniel. ECONOMICS OF PLANNED DEVELOPMENT. London: Estates Gazette, 1956. v, 152 p.

Lichfield, in this piece, first presents the conceptual development of the planning balance sheet method of evaluating urban development proposals.

Lichfield, Nathaniel; Kettle, Peter; and Whitbread, Michael. EVALUATION IN

THE PLANNING PROCESS. Oxford and New York: Pergamon Press, 1975. 326 p.

Limits its scope to evaluation of physical, development plans and programs. Within this context is the best review of all evaluation methods. Summarizes many of Lichfield's earlier work and references many other works. A number of case studies of evaluation. The essential text on this topic.

Nash, Christopher, et al. "Criteria for Evaluating Project Evaluation Techniques." JOURNAL OF AMERICAN INSTITUTE OF PLANNERS 41 (March 1975): 83-89.

The article examines the underlying value content of two program evaluation techniques: conventional (as opposed to social) cost-benefit analysis, and matrix evaluation. Stressed is the point that the results of evaluation depend on the underlying value judgments of the techniques.

Rivlin, Alice M. SYSTEMATIC THINKING FOR SOCIAL ACTION. Washington, D.C.: Brookings Institution, 1971. 150 p.

In this book, the author reviews (as of 1970) the progress made by evaluators of social programs in improving their methods. In addition to making a number of suggestions for improvement, she argues strongly for more "systematic experimentation."

Rothenberg, Jerome. ECONOMIC EVALUATION OF URBAN RENEWAL: CONCEPTUAL FOUNDATION OF BENEFIT-COST ANALYSIS. Washington, D.C.: Brookings Institution, 1967. 277 p.

An early attempt to apply cost-benefit analysis to physical development programs. Consideration given primarily to residential redevelopment. A narrow, limited, introductory analysis. Applied in a "crude, simplified" way to five Chicago projects.

Thomas, E[dwin].N., and Schofer, J[oseph].L. STRATEGIES FOR THE EVALUATION OF ALTERNATIVE TRANSPORTATION PLANS. National Cooperative Highway Research Program, Report no. 96. Washington, D.C.: Highway Research Board, National Research Council, 1970. 111 p.

A good concise document on the subject of plan evaluation—in this case, transportation plans. Concepts of plan evaluation are discussed, along with the relevant criteria for such evaluations. A practical, generalized framework for transportation plan evaluation.

3.4.2 Economic Evaluation Tools

Dorfman, Robert, ed. MEASURING BENEFITS OF GOVERNMENT INVESTMENTS. Washington, D.C.: Brookings Institution, 1965. 429 p.

This book contains seven papers commissioned for a conference at the Brookings Institution in 1963. Each focuses on the development and use of techniques for measuring the costs and benefits of public investment in different areas: research, recreation, education, transportation, urban renewal, and health. Included are criticisms of each of the papers.

Eckstein, Otto. WATER RESOURCE DEVELOPMENT. Cambridge, Mass.: Harvard University Press, 1958. 300 p.

In this book, a classic in benefit-cost (B/C) analysis, the author constructs a very sound theoretical basis for B/C analysis. He then goes on to apply the technique to a variety of water resource programs. A particularly valuable study for its rigorous examination of the theoretical base of B/C.

Goldman, Thomas A., ed. COST-EFFECTIVENESS ANALYSIS: NEW APPROACHES IN DECISION-MAKING. New York: Praeger, 1967. 231 p.

A good introduction to cost-effectiveness (C/E) analysis. The collection of thirteen papers is largely focused on military examples and case studies. It is useful for its general introduction to concepts, however, and does contain several chapters of direct relevance to public sector analysis.

Haveman, Robert H. ECONOMIC PERFORMANCE OF PUBLIC INVESTMENTS: AN EX POST EVALUATION OF WATER RESOURCE INVESMENTS. Baltimore, Md.: Johns Hopkins Press, 1972. 152 p.

In this book, Haveman makes the case for ex post analysis of earlier public projects using current cost-benefit (C/B) analytical procedures and original data. He offers a conceptual framework for such analysis and a review of the issues surrounding C/B analysis.

Hinrichs, H.H., and Taylor, G.M. PROGRAM BUDGETING AND BENEFIT-COST ANALYSIS. Pacific Palisades, Calif.: Goodyear, 1969. 420 p.

Provides a broad range of text, readings, and cases on cost-benefit analysis. The theoretical underpinnings of program budgeting and cost-benefit analysis are first examined. Then readings discuss some of the issues surrounding the use of the tools. Finally, a number of open-ended case studies are offered, many of which might prove useful in the classroom.

_____. SYSTEMATIC ANALYSIS: A PRIMER ON BENEFIT-COST ANALYSIS AND PROGRAM EVALUATION. Pacific Palisades, Calif.: Goodyear, 1972. 152 p.

Quick-and-dirty review of cost-benefit program analytic techniques. Geared to show "how it is done" with a number of complete case studies: mental health, recreation, education, defense, public safety, renewal, and criminal justice.

Methods and Techniques

Krutilla, John, and Eckstein, Otto. MULTIPLE PURPOSE RIVER DEVELOP-
MENT. Baltimore, Md.: Johns Hopkins Press, 1958. 301 p.

> The water resource area was really the first substantive area to be
> subjected to cost-benefit analysis. Concepts as well as cases
> developed much earlier and at a higher level of sophistication
> than other substantive areas. This work was a pioneering effort
> at applying concepts of cost-benefit analysis to water resource
> problems. Good theoretical presentation. Four solid case studies.

Lyden, Fremont, and Miller, Ernest, eds. PLANNING, PROGRAMMING,
BUDGETING: A SYSTEMS APPROACH TO MANAGEMENT. 2d ed. Chicago:
Markham, 1972. 423 p.

> This is a reader which focuses on the issues surrounding the imple-
> mentation of planning-programming-budgeting systems at both the
> federal and local levels. By 1972, some disenchantment with
> PPBS had set in, and the papers begin to reflect this. This is
> not a theoretical/conceptual work but is rather issue-oriented.
> Twenty-one papers include a number of substantive case studies.

McKean, Roland N. EFFICIENCY IN GOVERNMENT THROUGH SYSTEMS
ANALYSIS. New York: Wiley, 1958. 336 p.

> One of the first and clearest expositions of the cost-benefit analy-
> sis technique. The book is aimed at those interested in doing
> C/B analysis--it has a wide audience. Both the conceptual frame-
> work and the details of operation of the method are provided. Two
> applications examples are provided, both from water resources prob-
> lems. Though the literature of B/C has grown large, this book
> remains quite useful.

Merewitz, Leonard, and Sosnick, Stephen. THE BUDGET'S NEW CLOTHES:
A CRITIQUE OF PLANNING-PROGRAMMING-BUDGETING AND BENEFIT-
COST ANALYSIS. Chicago: Markham, 1971. 318 p.

> This is one of the first books published that was highly critical of
> the use of planning-programming-budgeting systems (PPBS). At
> publishing time, the federal government had just scaled down its
> PPBS effort. The book discusses the five elements of PPBS and
> describes the procedure used. An evaluation of that effort is
> then made. Cost-benefit analysis is also covered in some detail.
> Two case studies are also included.

Mishan, E.J. COST BENEFIT ANALYSIS. New and expanded ed. New
York: Praeger, 1976. xx, 454 p.

> An excellent introductory textbook on cost-benefit analysis. Most
> other texts on C/B are not nearly as inclusive or readable as this
> one. Eminently readable with a modicum of economics and
> statistics in one's background. Good examples. An excellent text.

Novick, David, ed. CURRENT PRACTICE IN PROGRAM BUDGETING (PPBS): ANALYSIS AND CASE STUDIES COVERING GOVERNMENT AND BUSINESS. New York: Crane, Russak, 1973. 242 p.

This book was written in order to update the experience with program budgeting. It is made up of twenty-one essays prepared largely by practitioners of program budgeting who describe their various experiences. These essays are introduced by five introductory chapters which describe the context of the use of program budgeting. There are a number of case studies here, including nine national governments, two states, and a number of local governments and private businesses.

_____. PROGRAM BUDGETING-PROGRAM ANALYSIS AND THE FEDERAL BUDGET. Cambridge, Mass.: Harvard University Press, 1965. 382 p.

This is a collection of readings that was published just as President Johnson announced the inauguration of program budgeting in the federal bureaucracy. The papers largely deal with issues surrounding the implementation of planning-programming-budgeting systems (PPBS) at the federal level. Six chapters deal each with different substantive areas, such as education.

Peters, G.H. COST-BENEFIT ANALYSIS AND PUBLIC EXPENDITURE. 3d ed. London: Institute of Economic Affairs, 1973. 76 p.

This is an excellent introduction to the economic principles which underlie cost-benefit analysis. The author updates the comprehensive review of the range of issues involved in using C/B done by Prest and Turvey in 1965. Concise, clear, and well written.

_____. "Land Use Studies in Britain: A Review of the Literature with Special Reference to Applications of Cost-Benefit Analysis." JOURNAL OF AGRICULTURAL ECONOMICS 21 (1970): 171-214.

An extensive review of applications of cost-benefit analysis in land-use allocation in Great Britain.

Prest, A.R., and Turvey, R. "Cost-Benefit Analysis: A Survey." ECONOMIC JOURNAL 75 (1965): 683-735.

The authors discuss the use of cost-benefit analysis (up to 1965) in a number of fields: water supply, transportation, land use, urban renewal, recreation, health, education, research and development, and defense. Excellent review, pre-1965.

Tietz, Michael B. "Cost Effectiveness: A Systems Approach to Analysis of Urban Services." JOURNAL OF AMERICAN INSTITUTE OF PLANNERS 34 (September 1968): 303-11.

The use of cost-effectiveness in analyzing public services is intro-

duced. The traditional use of performance measures and standards
is criticized, and new kinds of measures are discussed.

3.4.3 Policy Analysis and Social Program Evaluation

Blair, Louis H., and Schwartz, Alfred I. HOW CLEAN IS OUR CITY: A
GUIDE FOR MEASURING THE EFFECTIVENESS OF SOLID WASTE COLLEC-
TION ACTIVITIES. Washington, D.C.: Urban Institute, 1972. 67 p.

This is one of a number of studies on developing methodologies
for evaluating local government services by the Urban Institute.
It is an excellent introduction to a specific program evaluation--
in this case, solid waste. The level of material is quite easily
understood and concisely presented.

Caro, Francis G., ed. READINGS IN EVALUATION RESEARCH. New York:
Russell Sage Foundation, 1971. 418 p.

In a sense, this edited reader (31 articles) is a companion to Suchman's EVALUATIVE RESEARCH. The editor has allocated each
article to one of three sections: the basic issues, the organizational context for evaluation, and methodological issues. The
subject matter of most articles is centered on social action programs and social programs in general.

Hatry, Harry P., and Dunn, Diana R. MEASURING THE EFFECTIVENESS OF
LOCAL GOVERNMENT SERVICES: RECREATION. Washington, D.C.: Urban
Institute, 1971. 47 p.

An excellent example of a volume designed to aid local decision
makers on evaluating local programs--in this case, recreation programs. Good measures of effectiveness are offered as well as a
discussion of the issues surrounding their use. A limited, though
useful, bibliography is included.

Hatry, Harry P., et al. PRACTICAL PROGRAM EVALUATION FOR STATE
AND LOCAL GOVERNMENT OFFICIALS. Washington, D.C.: Urban Institute,
1973. 133 p.

This is an elementary introduction to program evaluation methodology, aimed at local government officials. Descriptions of several
different research designs, and a case study (sanitation). Reason-
ably good bibliography.

Reiner, Janet S., et al. "Client Analysis and the Planning of Public Programs."
JOURNAL OF AMERICAN INSTITUTE OF PLANNERS 29 (November 1963):
270-82.

The authors provide a neat conceptual step-by-step process for
determining social program design. These steps use the following

data on the target community: needs, eligibility, service rendered to clients, need satisfaction or benefits resulting. Clear conceptual statement with operational problems.

Russell, John R. CASES IN URBAN MANAGEMENT. Cambridge: MIT Press, 1974. 556 p.

This is a case book intended for classroom use with graduate students in urban planning and urban management. An accompanying set of teaching notes is available from the author. The content concerns the delivery of urban services--housing, sanitation, safety, health--and the tools used in the analysis of those service delivery systems. Light on quantitative methods; heavy on institutional contexts.

Schwab, Gerald, ed. EVALUATION HANDBOOK. 2d ed. Washington, D.C.: Agency for International Development, Office of Program Evaluation, 1972. 113 p.

A very concise look at the official program evaluation handbook of AID. Geared to the evaluation of "development" projects which include social as well as physical elements. Good summary document of field techniques.

Suchman, Edward A. EVALUATIVE RESEARCH: PRINCIPLES AND PRACTICE IN PUBLIC SERVICE AND SOCIAL ACTION PROGRAMS. New York: Russell Sage Foundation, 1967. 186 p.

This is one of the classics of social program evaluation. It is divided into three main sections which cover the conceptual, methodological, and administrative aspects of program evaluation. The methodological section includes an analysis of various research designs applicable to evaluative research.

Weiss, Carol H. EVALUATING ACTION PROGRAMS: READINGS IN SOCIAL ACTION AND EDUCATION. Boston: Allyn and Bacon, 1972. 365 p.

This book is intended primarily for helping evaluators conduct studies of action programs, primarily social services. It is not, however, a "how-to" book. It deals with contextual constraints and suggests alternative strategies of design, measurement, structure, relationship, and communication. It is a reader with twenty papers drawn from a number of substantive areas and an excellent introduction which compares and contrasts the individual papers.

_____. EVALUATION RESEARCH: METHODS OF ASSESSING PROGRAM EFFECTIVENESS. Englewood Cliffs, N.J.: Prentice-Hall, 1972. 160 p.

This is an introductory textbook on social program evaluation. Programs of interest include education, social work, corrections, health, mental health, job training, community action, and law.

It is aimed at the senior undergraduate or graduate student level for persons with an acquaintance with basic research methods, but not necessarily strong statistical skills. No full case studies. Good references, now somewhat dated.

Wholey, Joseph S., et al. FEDERAL EVALUATION POLICY: ANALYZING THE EFFECTS OF PUBLIC PROGRAMS. Washington, D.C.: Urban Institute, 1970. 134 p.

In late 1968, the Urban Institute undertook a review of program and project evaluation procedures used by a number of federal agencies. This book reports their findings and presents their recommendations for improving evaluation procedures in these agencies. In doing so, it displays many of the problems inherent in program evaluation.

Williams, Walter. SOCIAL POLICY RESEARCH AND ANALYSIS: THE EXPERIENCE IN THE FEDERAL SOCIAL AGENCIES. New York: Elsevier, 1971. 204 p.

This book concentrates on policy making at the federal level, largely during the War on Poverty years. It points out the lack of relevance of social science research to policy making--especially the failure of institutionalized policy analysis. It is rich in case-study material, but the cases concern the use of social science largely at the national level.

3.4.4 Impact Analysis

Burchell, Robert W., and Listokin, David. THE ENVIRONMENTAL IMPACT HANDBOOK. New Brunswick, N.J.: Rutgers University Center for Urban Policy Research, 1975. 231 p.

This book deals almost entirely with the environmental impact statement (EIS) and the procedural requirements established by various agencies. Its audience is primarily developers seeking HUD approvals who need a handbook of procedures. However, it does assume a working knowledge of the federal EIS requirement. Three appendixes provide critical background material.

Hefferman, Patrick, and Corwin, Rutham, eds. ENVIRONMENTAL IMPACT ASSESSMENT. San Francisco: Freeman, Cooper, 1975. 277 p.

Broader in scope than other books about EIS, this work discusses environmental impact assessment and the potential of EIS as a planning tool. It places EIS in a social and legislative context and, as a reader, exposes a number of critical issues surrounding EIS and its implications for planning.

Muller, Thomas. FISCAL IMPACTS OF LAND DEVELOPMENT: A CRITIQUE

OF METHODS AND REVIEW OF ISSUES. Washington, D.C.: Urban Institute, 1975. 60 p.

This study evaluated many recent studies of the fiscal impacts of land use change. Analyzes the state-of-the-art of fiscal impact studies. Comprehensive bibliography.

Real Estate Research Corp. THE COSTS OF SPRAWL: DETAILED COST ANAL-YSIS. Washington, D.C.: Superintendent of Documents, 1974. 278 p.

This is the companion volume to RERC's literature review, and it gives a detailed analysis of the costs of six prototype housing patterns and six prototype development patterns. Similar costs are presented for different types of commercial development.

Rosen, Sherman J. MANUAL FOR ENVIRONMENTAL IMPACT EVALUATION. Englewood Cliffs, N.J.: Prentice-Hall, 1976. 232 p.

This is a basic guide to the preparation of an EIS. The National Environmental Policy Act (NEPA) is detailed and then explained thoroughly, along with legal interpretations. A variety of approaches to impact assessment are discussed, and seven appendixes including a copy of NEPA and A-95 guidelines are included, along with a sample draft EIS.

Schaenman, Philip S., and Muller, Thomas. MEASURING IMPACTS OF LAND DEVELOPMENT: AN INITIAL APPROACH. Washington, D.C.: Urban Institute, 1975. 93 p.

This is an initial, exploratory effort to examine ways to evaluate proposed development projects, aimed largely at local decision makers. The study describes forty-eight impact measures grouped into five impact areas: local economy, natural environment, aesthetic and cultural values, public and private services, and housing and social conditions. It then analyzes these measures critically and demonstrates their use on case projects.

3.4.5 Land Use Planning and Law

American Public Health Association. PLANNING THE NEIGHBORHOOD. Chicago: Public Administration Service, 1960. 94 p.

This document is a classic of the "craft" stage of the planning profession's development. It contains standards to be used by planners in the design and layout of residential neighborhoods. It was, in its time, one of the few basic references planners used in their work, which was almost entirely physical design and planning.

Babcock, Richard F. THE ZONING GAME. Madison: University of Wisconsin Press, 1966. xvi, 202 p.

One of the more important books dealing with zoning from the
viewpoint of practices and policies. The perspective here is more
towards the players and rules of the zoning game rather than
legal analysis. As such, it is most useful.

Bair, Frederick H., and Bartley, Ernest R. TEXT OF A MODEL ZONING
ORDINANCE WITH COMMENTARY. Chicago: American Society of Planning
Officials, 1965. 20 p.

A standard reference work which supplies most of the details needed
for small and medium-sized cities. The model zoning ordinance is
quite common in law practice and still prevalent in land use controls. This is the most common version.

Bartholomew, Harland. LAND USES IN AMERICAN CITIES. Cambridge,
Mass.: Harvard University Press, 1955. 168 p.

The foundation for much land use scholarship that followed, this
volume described the use of land in fifty-three central cities and
thirty-three satellite cities in the United States. Primarily descriptive in nature, it also describes the techniques used in developing a land use survey.

Bassett, Edward H. ZONING: THE LAWS, ADMINISTRATION AND COURT
DECISIONS DURING THE FIRST TWENTY YEARS. New York: Russell Sage
Foundation, 1936. 275 p.

The first serious evaluation of how zoning was working in the
United States. Bassett is one of the founders of the planning
movement and tended to be somewhat zealous in his advocacy
of zoning, but nonetheless this is solid history.

Beuscher, J.H., ed. LAND USE CONTROLS--CASES AND MATERIALS. Madison, Wis.: College Printing and Typing Company, 1964. 557 p.

The class materials and textbook by the master of land use controls
education. Beuscher's work has never really been improved upon,
and these materials are still a classic. Difficult to obtain, but
still invaluable.

Chapin, F. Stuart, Jr. "Taking Stock of Techniques for Shaping Urban Growth."
JOURNAL OF AMERICAN INSTITUTE OF PLANNERS 24 (May 1963): 76-87.

In this article, the most important figure in American land use
planning described his techniques for guiding urban growth. They
included the general plan as an organizing element, an urban
development policies instrument, an area-wide public works program, an urban development code, and an educational program
for the public.

_____. URBAN LAND USE PLANNING. 2d ed. Urbana: University of

Illinois Press, 1965. xvi, 482 p.

The first edition of this book was a handbook which gave every step in the plan-making process--an exemplary state-of-the-land-use-planning-art, circa mid-1950s. This second edition updates the first by acknowledging the infusion of urban and regional theory into planning--and the consequent changes in perspective. The book is divided into three parts: location theory, urban structural analysis, and plan making. A classic work.

Clawson, Marion, and Hall, Peter. PLANNING AND URBAN GROWTH: AN ANGLO-AMERICAN COMPARISON. Baltimore, Md.: Johns Hopkins Press, 1973. xii, 300 p.

A very interesting comparison of planning for urban growth and change in the United States as contrasted to England. There is much skepticism in this book as to the transferability and success in either country. It constitutes a case comparative study.

Clawson, Marion, and Steward, Charles L. LAND USE INFORMATION: A CRITICAL SURVEY OF U.S. STATISTICS INCLUDING POSSIBILITIES FOR GREATER UNIFORMITY. Baltimore, Md.: Johns Hopkins Press, 1966. 402 p.

This is a book about land use information, its collection and use. Contained in the volume is a survey of the state of land use statistics in the United States, followed by a plea for greater uniformity in data collection techniques and a proposal for a land use classification system.

Costonis, John J. SPACE ADRIFT: LANDMARK PRESERVATION AND THE MARKET PLACE. Urbana: University of Illinois Press, 1974. xx, 207 p.

Costonis relies on the legal concept of transferability of development rights to develop a fascinating approach to historic preservation. The case study of Chicago is used heavily as the best example of the process and techniques. While somewhat complex, he argues that such an approach is actually lucrative to developers.

Delafons, John. LAND USE CONTROLS IN THE UNITED STATES. Cambridge, Mass.: Harvard University Press, 1962.

Somewhat dated, but still one of the better treatments of land use controls. The book is primarily a text for early courses on land use controls, and it is strong on evolution of concepts and precedents.

Dolgin, E.L., and Guilbert, T., eds. FEDERAL ENVIRONMENTAL LAW. St. Paul, Minn.: West, 1974. xxxvii, 1,600 p.

A detailed yet not overbearing summary of the scope, context, and meaning of the large body of federal law concerning such environmental problems as air, water, and land. This book deals heavily with case histories and may be difficult for the nonlawyer or nontechnician.

Haar, Charles M. LAND-USE PLANNING. Boston: Little, Brown, 1959.
With periodic supplements. xxxv, 764 p.

> The curious title masks the basic textbook on land use controls.
> It deals with all of the basic tools, including zoning, subdivision
> regulation, official map, role of master plans, and housing regu-
> lations. Supplements help to update concepts.

Kent, T.J. URBAN GENERAL PLAN. San Francisco: Chandler, 1964.
xviii, 210 p.

> This is a book about the "master plan" and a vigorous defense of
> its use as a major tool of planning. It was published at a time
> when that concept had begun to come under severe attack, es-
> pecially because the social (as opposed to physical) aspects of
> cities were generally ignored by "the plan." Kent ignored that
> criticism and didn't deal with it. In addition, he proposed a
> new client for "the plan"--that is, the legislative body of each
> city. This book is a classic.

Lyle, John, and von Wodtke, Mark. "An Information System for Environmental Planning." JOURNAL OF AMERICAN INSTITUTE OF PLANNERS 40
(November 1974): 394-413.

> The authors report on the development of an information system
> developed for San Diego County which aids in environmental
> planning. The system, though computer-oriented, can be used
> manually.

Mandelker, Daniel R. ENVIRONMENTAL AND LAND CONTROLS LEGISLA-
TION. Indianapolis: Bobbs-Merrill, 1976. ix, 417 p.

> An excellent book on the most recent developments in legislation
> pertaining to land development controls, environmental impact
> statements, air and water quality programs, and coastal zone
> management. There is an outstanding chapter on the Hawaii
> experience and a chapter on Vermont written by David G. Heeter.

Mausel, Paul W., et al. "Regional Land Use Classification Derived from
Computer-Processed Satellite Data." JOURNAL OF AMERICAN INSTITUTE
OF PLANNERS 42 (March 1976): 153-64.

> The article introduces the use of multispectral data from an earth
> orbiting satellite for developing a regional land use inventory.
> Differences between this approach and the on-site survey and
> aerial photo interpretation approaches are discussed.

Public Administration Service. ACTION FOR CITIES: A GUIDE FOR COM-
MUNITY PLANNING. Chicago: 1943. 77 p.

> Another of the comprehensive planning sources that appeared near
> the end of World War II, this document presents a procedure for

planning for communities. Included are sections on reconnaissance as well as plan development. Not intended as a detailed "how-to" manual, it was a generalized approach to physical planning for communities. Not a "standards" text.

Scott, Randall W., ed. MANAGEMENT AND CONTROL OF GROWTH. 3 vols. Washington, D.C.: Urban Land Institute, 1975.

This is virtually an encyclopedia of the growth management move-ment in the United States. Well over a hundred articles deal with every conceivable issue of growth controls. There may be a tinge of suburban orientation and compromise in the work, but it is unique.

Smith, Herbert H. THE CITIZEN'S GUIDE TO ZONING. West Trenton, N.J.: Chandler-Davis, 1965. 182 p.

A curious little book which is intended to present the basic con-cepts of zoning to citizens in small and medium-sized cities. It is valuable because there has been no other comparable title nor level of detail developed since then.

Urban Land Institute. THE COMMUNITY BUILDERS HANDBOOK. Washing-ton, D.C.: 1960. 476 p.

This is a basic compilation of standards, models, and recommended service levels. It is intended to be a basic reference for planners and developers dealing with new communities and subdivisions.

Way, Douglas. TERRAIN ANALYSIS: A GUIDE TO SITE SELECTION USING AERIAL PHOTOGRAPHIC INTERPRETATION. Stroudsburg, Pa.: Dowden, Hutchinson, and Ross, 1973. 392 p.

An elementary text on the subject and relevance to site selection and environmental evaluation. Good examples, well illustrated. Explains what the method can be used for, and the possible results.

Williams, Norman. AMERICAN LAND PLANNING LAW. 5 vols. Chicago: Callaghan, 1974.

The major definitive, perhaps exhaustive, treatment of land use controls. The five volumes cover every form of controls with his-torical, substantive, and case studies. Williams has a remarkable ability to blend planning and law, which is not always found in such works.

3.4.6 Urban Economics, Capital Budgeting, and Finance

Coughlin, Robert E. "The Capital Programming Problem." JOURNAL OF AMERICAN INSTITUTE OF PLANNERS 26 (February 1960): 39-48.

Methods and Techniques

In this article, the author, a staff member of the Philadelphia City Planning Commission, sets out an analytic framework for formulating a capital program given a comprehensive plan. This is, in part, derived from his experience in Philadelphia. There is not a great deal of literature available on this topic.

Coughlin, Robert E., and Pitts, Charles A. "The Capital Programming Process." JOURNAL OF AMERICAN INSTITUTE OF PLANNERS 26 (August 1960): 236-41.

As a followup to an earlier article, this one describes the actors involved and the process of capital programming—again from the experience of the Philadelphia City Planning Commission.

Crecine, John P., ed. FINANCING THE METROPOLIS; PUBLIC POLICY IN URBAN ECONOMIES. Urban Affairs Annual Reviews, vol. 4. Beverly Hills, Calif.: Sage, 1970. 632 p.

This book contains twenty articles divided into the following categories: The Urban Economic System, Public Expenditures, The Economy of the Poor in an Urban Setting, The Provision and Delivery of Urban Services, and Budgetary Reform and the Restructuring of Public Expenditure Determinants. In this latter section are contained papers by Mushkin, Bount, and Meltsner and Wildavsky which both introduce and criticize the use of PPBS in cities.

Haveman, Robert [H.]. THE ECONOMICS OF THE PUBLIC SECTOR. New York: Wiley, 1970. 225 p.

An excellent introduction to the theory of public sector financing and spending. Provides a theoretical framework within which problems of public expenditures can be examined. Though largely aimed at the national level, many of the principles apply to public expenditure analysis at the local level.

Haveman, Robert [H.], and Margolis, Julius, eds. PUBLIC EXPENDITURES AND POLICY ANALYSIS. Chicago: Markham, 1970. 596 p.

Contained in this reader are twenty-five papers focused on public expenditure economics. The material is mixed between theoretical and applied, with a number of papers aimed at issues surrounding the use of benefit-cost analysis (i.e. discount rate, shadow pricing, uncertainty, etc.). There are six chapters devoted to analyzing the experience with planning-programming-budgeting systems in several departments of the federal government. Many classical papers here.

Hirsch, Werner Z. THE ECONOMICS OF STATE AND LOCAL GOVERNMENT. New York: McGraw-Hill, 1970. 333 p.

A comprehensive review of analytic techniques used in examining the provision of public services: assessment of demand, financing, production, distribution, and budgeting. Also contains abbreviated summaries of the applications of the analytic tools.

_____, ed. REGIONAL ACCOUNTS FOR POLICY DECISIONS. Baltimore, Md.: Johns Hopkins Press, 1966. 230 p.

This is the third volume in the regional accounts series of Resources for the Future. It is an eclectic collection of papers with a focus on information collection and handling for a number of public systems: urban renewal, schools, economic development, and state and regional planning.

Margolis, Julius, ed. THE PUBLIC ECONOMY OF URBAN COMMUNITIES; PAPERS. Washington, D.C.: Resources for the Future, distributed by Johns Hopkins Press, 1965. 264 p.

This book contains eleven papers presented at the second conference on urban public expenditures sponsored by Resources for the Future in 1964. The papers are diverse but are all aimed at the development of analytic tools which aid in studying urban public expenditures. They are largely economic in nature, with several of them being unavailable elsewhere.

Mushkin, Selma J. "P.P.B. for the Cities: Problems and the Next Steps." In FINANCING THE METROPOLIS, edited by John P. Crecine, pp. 247-84. Urban Affairs Annual Reviews, vol. 4. Beverly Hills, Calif.: Sage, 1970

At the time of this writing, this article was both critical and optimistic in its assessment of the potential applicability of PPBS in local government. It describes some aspects of the system in detail and includes an appendix with a list of cities attempting to implement the system, circa 1969. An excellent introduction to the topic.

Perloff, Harvey [S.], and Wingo, Lowdon, [Jr.], eds. ISSUES IN URBAN ECONOMICS. Baltimore, Md.: Johns Hopkins Press, for Resources of the Future, 1968. 668 p.

This is a reader in urban economics containing twelve papers and followup comments. Though strictly speaking this is not a "methodology" book, it contains a number of articles whose thrust is urban analysis. They often contain urban economic analytical techniques useful to the planner. See especially the papers by Thompson, Sonenblum, Muth, and Harris.

Pfouts, Ralph W., ed. THE TECHNIQUES OF URBAN ECONOMIC ANALYSIS. West Trenton, N.J.: Chandler-David, 1960. 410 p.

This is a book of twenty-one well-known articles concerning the economic base concept: historical development, theory, application, and the benefits and costs of its use in planning. Many important authors, including Andrews, Tiebout, Grigsby, Hoyt, Hirsch, and Isard. The book also contains material on input-output analysis and interregional trade, as alternatives to economic base analysis. Almost all articles are reprints of important (and previously scattered) journal articles.

Schaller, Howard, ed. PUBLIC EXPENDITURE DECISIONS IN THE URBAN COMMUNITY. Washington, D.C.: Resources for the Future, distributed by Johns Hopkins Press, 1963. ix, 198 p.

This volume contains the proceedings of a 1962 RFF conference held to "assess the state of the art of applying the tools of economic analysis to the public sector of the urban economy." The book generally can be divided into two parts: background papers on facets of urban expenditures, and papers which describe methods (and concepts) relevant to the "hows" of public-expenditure decision making. Many classic papers.

Thompson, Wilbur R. A PREFACE TO URBAN ECONOMICS. Baltimore, Md.: Johns Hopkins Press, 1965. 432 p.

Written to be the textbook in urban, as opposed to regional, economics, the book was destined to be a seminal work. And it was one. However, Thompson does concentrate more on interurban (regional) as opposed to strictly intraurban economics, rationalizing this interest as growth management as the solution to urban problems. Those seeking local insights and solutions to economic problems will be disappointed. A number of excellent chapters, however.

Tiebout, Charles M. THE COMMUNITY ECONOMIC BASE STUDY. Supplementary Paper 16. New York: Committee for Economic Development, 1962. 84 p.

This is the classic work on this topic, and it remains so today. Aimed at laypersons, it is easy to read and understand with a minimal background in economics. Taking a nuts-and-bolts approach, the author lays out the steps in conducting a study of this kind, explaining its inherent weaknesses along the way.

Chapter 4
RELATED REFERENCES

In order to provide additional references, we have selected a brief list of representative bibliographies and journals. These simply represent some of the more important and recent listings. This selection is by no means exhaustive but could be considered to be fairly typical of what is available. It should be noted that the Council of Planning Librarians has a considerable and extensive list of bibliographies, some annotated, pertaining to many areas of urban planning. While uneven in quality, these bibliographies should be useful when seeking information on specific topics in urban planning.

4.1 RELATED BIBLIOGRAPHIES AND REFERENCES

Ashworth, Graham. ENCYCLOPEDIA OF PLANNING. London: Barrie and Jenkins, 1973. 120 p.

> A British-oriented glossary of planning terms, with biographies of significant individuals in the British planning tradition. Also includes brief descriptions and illustrations of particular "model" cities.

Bestor, George C., and Jones, Holway R. CITY PLANNING: A BASIC BIBLIOGRAPHY OF SOURCES AND TRENDS. Sacramento: California Council of Civil Engineers and Land Surveyors, 1962. xv, 195 p.

> An excellent bibliography for its time which, when read at present, gives one a sense of the definition of planning, circa 1962. Annotations appear where appropriate. Good indexes.

Branch, Melville C. SELECTED REFERENCES FOR CORPORATE PLANNING. New York: American Management Association, 1966. 191 p. Paperbound.

> An annotated bibliography containing five hundred entries, arranged in two general sections--"Nature, Purpose and Process of Planning" and "Theory and Techniques of Planning Analysis"--and five functional planning sections. Its usefulness today is limited because of its out-of-date entries and the arbitrary nature of many of its selections.

Related References

Brennan, Maribeth. PERT AND CPM: A SELECTED BIBLIOGRAPHY. Vol. 53. Monticello, Ill.: Council of Planning Librarians, 1968. 11 p.

This is an unannotated bibliography about the Program Evaluation Review Technique (PERT) and the Critical Path Method (CPM) and their usefulness to planning and transportation projects.

Chapin, F. Stuart, Jr. SELECTED REFERENCES ON URBAN PLANNING CONCEPTS AND METHODS. Chapel Hill: Department of City and Regional Planning, University of North Carolina, 1972. 83 p.

A group of books, reports, and articles that represent a wide range of methods. The concepts and methods are largely related to physical planning and land development, and they are useful in this context.

Cherukapolle, Nirmala divi. APPLICATION OF MULTIVARIATE STATISTICAL METHODS TO URBAN AND REGIONAL PLANNING. Vol. 136. Monticello, Ill.: Council of Planning Librarians, 1970. 12 p.

With occasional annotation, this bibliography covers books and articles which demonstrate the use of multivariate methods in planning. Many of the readings cited are in the field of geography and they relate to urban structure.

Clark, Robert A. DATA BANK ON INFORMATION SYSTEMS PUBLICATIONS --WITH EMPHASIS ON LAND USE. Vol. 59. Monticello, Ill.: Council of Planning Librarians, 1968. 10 p.

This is a bibliography with a solid introduction to the state-of-the-art as of 1968. It is not annotated.

Dickey, John W. URBAN LAND USE MODELS BIBLIOGRAPHY. Vol. 959. Monticello, Ill.: Council of Planning Librarians, 1976. 33 p.

The author references and cross-references 390 bibliographic items by subject with reference to models, by the subject matter of specific models, and by specific important models themselves. A good source to the literature of specific models.

Giarrantani, Frank, et al. REGIONAL AND INTERREGIONAL INPUT-OUTPUT ANALYSIS: AN ANNOTATED BIBLIOGRAPHY. Morgantown: West Virginia University Library, 1976. 127 p.

An excellent annotated bibliography which covers the theoretical as well as applied literature on regional as well as interregional input-output analysis. Input-output studies not focused on regional issues were omitted. Outstanding source book.

Hebert, Budd H. STOCHASTIC PROGRAMMING: A SELECTED BIBLIOGRAPHY. Vol. 132. Monticello, Ill.: Council of Planning Librarians, 1970. 23 p.

This is an annotated bibliography, largely focusing on theoretical issues since application to planning problems has been minimal. It is divided into three parts: linear programming, chance and constrained programming, and distributional problems.

Lightwood, Martha B. PUBLIC AND BUSINESS PLANNING IN THE UNITED STATES: A BIBLIOGRAPHY. Management Information Guide No. 26. Detroit: Gale Research, 1972. 309 p.

A useful guide to information sources, particularly for sectoral planning in private business. Well-developed sections include economic planning, managerial and organizational planning, financial planning, R&D planning, and business forecasting. Includes lists of planning bibliographies, statistical sources, and periodicals.

McLaughlin, James F. APPLICATION OF LINEAR PROGRAMMING TO URBAN PLANNING. Vol. 45. Monticello, Ill.: Council of Planning Librarians, 1968. 4 p.

Contained in the abstract of the author's thesis and a number of citations to books and articles which relate linear programming to urban planning.

Miller, Donald H. PLANNING EVALUATION: A SELECTIVE BIBLIOGRAPHY ON BENEFIT-COST, GOAL-ACHIEVEMENT, AND RELATED ANALYTICAL METHODS. Vol. 935. Monticello, Ill.: Council of Planning Librarians, 1975. 37 p.

This bibliography cites works concerned with the a priori evaluation of largely physical, development plans. Evaluation of social programs is not treated here. Methods include cost-benefit, cost-effectiveness, cost-revenue, and goals-achievement analysis, among others. Citations to case studies are included.

Mitchell, Bruce, and Mitchell, Joan. BENEFIT-COST ANALYSIS: A SELECT BIBLIOGRAPHY. Vol. 267. Monticello, Ill.: Council of Planning Librarians, 1972. 44 p.

This is an extensive bibliography, largely not annotated, which covers both the background and application of B/C analysis. The applications section is broken down into six subsections. They are regional planning and resource management, urban, transportation, human resources, recreation, and water.

Neroda, Edward W. OPERATIONS RESEARCH: AN ELEMENTARY GUIDE TO THE LITERATURE. Vol. 403. Monticello, Ill.: Council of Planning Librarians, 1973. 21 p.

Most entries are annotated. This is a directory of source materials in the field of operations research. It includes indexes, abstracts, bibliographies, dictionaries, directories, and other materials.

Related References

Rea, Louis M. REGIONAL SCIENCE: THEORY, APPLICATION AND POLICY.
Vol. 1080. Monticello, Ill.: Council of Planning Librarians, 1976. 41 p.

This is a very useful annotated bibliography intended as an introduction to the field. Thus, entries are chosen for their introductory character. The outline of the volume provides a good outline of the field itself.

Real Estate Research Corp. THE COSTS OF SPRAWL: LITERATURE REVIEW
AND BIBLIOGRAPHY. Washington, D.C.: Superintendent of Documents,
1974. 278 p.

An excellent source document on the various costs associated with
different patterns of residential development. Contains both a
literature review of the topic and an annotated bibliography. An
excellent essay on the economics and environmental effects of
development introduces this volume. A companion volume presents
detailed cost breakdowns of alternative residential housing and
development patterns.

Rooks, Dana C. PERT, PROGRAM EVALUATION AND REVIEW TECHNIQUE,
1962-1974: AN ANNOTATED BIBLIOGRAPHY. Vol. 958. Monticello, Ill.:
Council of Planning Librarians, 1976. 42 p.

In this bibliography, PERT is the only network technique covered.
It is divided into four parts: generalized descriptions, theory,
specific applications, evaluation and critiques.

Schlachter, Gail, and Belli, Donna. PROGRAM EVALUATION IN THE PUB-
LIC SECTOR: A SELECTED BIBLIOGRAPHY. Vol. 913. Monticello, Ill.:
Council of Planning Librarians, 1975. 26 p.

This bibliography deals largely with the evaluation of social programs. Literature on specific evaluations has been excluded as
well as reference materials such as statistical textbooks. Contained are citations on methods of program evaluation as well as
the political context of evaluation. See CPL Bibliography No.
975 for an annotated bibliography on the same topic.

Spielvogel, Samuel. A SELECTED BIBLIOGRAPHY ON CITY AND REGIONAL
PLANNING. Washington, D.C.: Scarecrow Press, 1951. 276 p.

A book with 2,182 annotated entries covering city and regional
planning in their widest aspects. As a result, each of these
facets, such as urban sociology, docks and harbors, and the United
Nations, is covered superficially with a few arbitrarily chosen
titles. This volume's date also limits its usefulness.

Steiber, Steven R. EVALUATION RESEARCH: A BIBLIOGRAPHIC OVERVIEW.
Vol. 975. Monticello, Ill.: Council of Planning Librarians, 1976. 41 p.

An annotated bibliography broken down into four sections which provide theoretically relevant sources and reference materials, methodologies, methodologies vis-à-vis substantive policy areas, and case studies. See CPL Bibliography No. 913 for an unannotated bibliography on the same subject.

Swanick, Eric L. PLANNING-PROGRAMMING-BUDGETING SYSTEMS (PPBS): A SELECTIVE BIBLIOGRAPHY, SUPPLEMENT TO CPL EXCHANGE BIBLIOGRAPHY NO. 289. Exchange Bibliography Vol. 778. Monticello, Ill.: Council of Planning Librarians, 1975. 16 p.

This bibliography, without categorization, rather unselectively supplements the earlier CPL bibliography on the topic. Literature is largely from 1971 to 1975.

Tucker, Dorothy. COMPUTERS AND INFORMATION SYSTEMS IN PLANNING AND RELATED GOVERNMENTAL FUNCTIONS. Exchange Bibliography Vol. 42. Monticello, Ill.: Council of Planning Librarians, 1968. 21 p.

This is a bibliography, without annotation, that covers July 1960 to December 1968 and updates Richard Duke's earlier bibliography which covered the topic up to 1960. Ten major topics, including state and local government, EDP, EDP in the planning agency, computer graphics, information retrieval, time sharing, and modeling.

Tudor, Dean. PLANNING-PROGRAMMING-BUDGETING SYSTEMS: REVISED EDITION INCLUDING EXCHANGE BIBLIOGRAPHIES 121 AND 183. Exchange Bibliography Vol. 289. Monticello, Ill.: Council of Planning Librarians, 1972. 28 p.

This is the most recent update of previous bibliographies on the topic. Largely unannotated, the thrust is in the application of PPBS within government.

White, Brenda. THE LITERATURE AND STUDY OF URBAN AND REGIONAL PLANNING. London: Routledge and Kegan Paul, 1974. 223 p.

This annotated bibliography has a British focus and covers the administration and content of planning. It includes a review of planning journals and a list of information sources, but its usefulness is limited by its many entries which are governmental or local planning studies of only specialized and transient interest.

Whittick, Arnold, ed. ENCYCLOPEDIA OF URBAN PLANNING. New York: McGraw-Hill, 1974. 1,218 p.

Formally, this encyclopedia is alphabetically organized. Conceptually, it covers planning legislation and administration; professional practice, education, and training; planning agencies and institutions; geography and climate; history and traditions of planning to the end of the nineteenth century, and in the twentieth century; new towns and communities; city and town extensions; and urban renewal. A traditional physical planning oriented compilation.

Related References

Williams, Richard C. THE SEARCH FOR A THEORY OF PLAN-MAKING METHOD: AN ANNOTATED BIBLIOGRAPHY. Vol. 781-782. Monticello, Ill.: Council of Planning Librarians, 1975. 90 p.

> Despite its promising title, this bibliography concentrates more on the literature of planning theory (the theoretical framework for planning) than on how planning is done analytically (planning method). Contained, though, are a number of references to major works in planning method.

4.2 JOURNALS AND PERIODICALS

1. Administration and Society. Beverly Hills, Calif.: Sage Publications, 1969-- . Quarterly.

2. Administrative Science Quarterly. Ithaca, N.Y.: Cornell University, Graduate School of Business and Public Administration, 1956-- .

3. AIA Journal. Washington, D.C.: American Institute of Architects, 1944-- . Monthly.

4. Annals of Regional Science. Bellingham, Wash.: Western Regional Science Association, 1967-- . 3 times a year.

5. Appraisal Journal. Chicago: American Institute of Real Estate Appraisers, National Association of Realtors, 1932-- . Quarterly.

6. Architectural Record. New York: McGraw-Hill, 1891-- . Monthly.

7. Behavioral Science. Louisville, Ky.: University of Louisville, Health Science Center Library, 1956-- . Bimonthly.

8. Built Environment. London: Godwin, 1937-- . Quarterly.

9. Comparative Urban Research. New York: City University of New York, Comparative Urban Studies Center, 1972-- . 3 times a year.

10. Contact in Urban and Regional Affairs. Waterloo, Ontario, Can.: University of Waterloo, Faculty of Environmental Studies, 1969-- . 6 times a year.

11. Design and Environment. New York: R.C. Publications, 1970-- . Quarterly.

12. Environmental Affairs. Brighton, Mass.: Boston College Law School, Environmental Law Center, 1971-- . Quarterly.

13. Environmental Science and Technology. Washington, D.C.: American Chemical Society, 1967-- . Monthly.

14. Environment and Behavior. Beverly Hills, Calif.: Sage Publications, 1969-- . Quarterly.

15. Environment and Planning A. London: Pion, 1969-- . 8 times a year.

16. Fordham Urban Law Journal. New York: Fordham University School of Law, 1972-- . 3 times a year.

17. Futures. Guilford, Surrey, Engl.: I.P.C. Science and Technology Press, 1968-- . Bimonthly.

18. Geographical Analysis. Columbus: Ohio State University Press, 1969-- . Quarterly.

19. Growth and Change. Lexington: University of Kentucky, College of Business and Economics, 1970-- . Quarterly.

20. Health Planning. New York: Comprehensive Health Planning Agency, 1969-- . Monthly.

21. Human Organization. Boulder: University of Colorado, Institute of Behavioral Science, 1941-- . Quarterly.

22. Journal of Environmental Economics and Management. New York: Academic Press, 1974-- . Quarterly.

23. Journal of Environmental Systems. Farmingdale, N.Y.: Baywood Publishing Co., 1971-- . Quarterly.

24. Journal of Housing. Washington, D.C.: National Association of Housing and Redevelopment Officials, 1944-- . 11 times a year.

25. Journal of Political Economy. Chicago: University of Chicago Press, 1892-- . Bimonthly.

26. Journal of Regional Science. Philadelphia: Regional Science Research Institute, 1958-- . 3 times a year.

27. Journal of Transport Economics and Policy. London: London School of Economics and Political Science, 1967-- . 3 times a year.

28. Journal of Urban Analysis. London: Gordon and Breach Science Publishers, 1972-- . 2 times a year.

29. Journal of Urban Economics. New York: Academic Press, 1974-- . Quarterly.

30. Land Economics. Madison: University of Wisconsin, 1925-- . Quarterly.

31. Long Range Planning. Elmsford, N.Y.: Pergamon Press, 1968-- . Bimonthly.

32. Planner. London: Royal Town Planning Institute, 1973-- . 10 times a year.

33. Planner. Brisbane, Australia: Royal Australian Planning Institute, n.d. 4 times a year.

34. Planning. Chicago: American Society of Planning Officials, 1935-- . Monthly.

35. Planning and Public Policy. Urbana: University of Illinois at Urbana-Champaign, Bureau of Urban and Regional Planning Research, 1975-- . Quarterly.

36. Planning Comment. Philadelphia: University of Pennsylvania, Student Planners Association, 1962-- . 2 times a year.

37. Planning Outlook. Newcastle upon Tyne, Engl.: University of Newcastle upon Tyne, Department of Town and Country Planning, 1948-- . 2 times a year.

Related References

38. Planning Review. New York: Crane, Russak and Co., 1973-- . Bi-monthly.

39. Policy Analysis. Berkeley and Los Angeles: University of California Press, 1975-- . Quarterly.

40. Political Science Quarterly. New York: Academy of Political Science, 1886-- .

41. Public Administration Review. Washington, D.C.: American Society for Public Administration, 1940-- . Bimonthly.

42. Public Interest. New York: National Affairs, 1965-- . Quarterly.

43. Real Estate Law Journal. Boston: Warren, Gorham and Lamont, 1972-- . Quarterly.

44. Real Estate Review. Boston: Warren, Gorham and Lamont, 1971-- . Quarterly.

45. Regional Science and Urban Economics. Amsterdam, Netherlands: North Holland Publishing Co., 1971-- . Quarterly.

46. Regional Studies. Elmsford, N.Y.: Pergamon Press, 1967-- . Quarterly.

47. Review of Regional Studies. Birmingham: University of Alabama, Southern Regional Science Association, 1970-- . 3 times a year.

48. Traffic Quarterly. Westport, Conn.: Eno Foundation for Transportation, 1973-- .

49. Transportation. Amsterdam, Netherlands: Elsevier Scientific Publishing Co., 1972-- . Quarterly.

50. Urban Affairs Quarterly. Beverly Hills, Calif.: Sage Publications, 1965-- . Quarterly.

51. Urban Studies. Edinburgh, Scotland: Longman Group, 1964-- . 3 times a year.

52. Water Resources Bulletin. Champaign, Ill.: American Water Resources Association, 1965-- . Bimonthly.

AUTHOR INDEX

In addition to authors, this index includes all editors, compilers, and translators cited in this text. References are to page numbers and alphabetization is letter by letter.

Author Index

Author Index

H

Haar, Charles M. 6, 43, 122
Hadley, G. 97
Haefele, Edwin T. 39
Hall, Peter 66, 121
Hallman, Howard W. 63
Hampden-Turner, Charles 63
Hanssmann, Fred 97
Hardin, Garrett 26
Harkell, Elizabeth 48
Harris, Britton 81, 101
Harrison, Bennett 6
Hartman, Chester W. 65
Hatry, Harry P. 93, 116
Haveman, Robert H. 113, 124
Hawley, Amos H. 6
Hearle, Edward 90
Heer, David M. 86
Hefferman, Patrick 118
Heikoff, Joseph M. 54
Hemmins, George 102
Henning, Dale A. 59
Herbert, Budd H. 128
Heskin, Allan 32
Heywood, Philip 36
Hickman, Bert G. 107
Hilberseimer, L. 2
Hilhorst, Jos. G.M. 49
Hill, Morris 111
Hilton, Peter 59
Hinrichs, H.H. 113
Hirsch, Werner Z. 54, 107, 124-25
Hirschman, Albert O. 72
Hirten, John E. 57
Hochwald, Werner 108
Hodge, Gerald 94
Hoffman, George W. 67
Holleb, Doris B. 86
Hoos, Ida R. 90
Hoover, Edgar M. 108
Horton, Frank E. 106
Howard, Ebenezer 8-9
Howard, John T. 54
Howe, Charles W. 96
Howel, Brandon 69
Hoyt, Homer 108
Hudson, Barclay M. 31, 111
Huff, Darrell 94
Hughes, J.T. 111

Hughes, James W. 8, 84
Hyman, Drew 65

I

International City Management Association 84, 87
Isard, Walter 108-9, 126

J

Jacobs, Jane 7
Jacobsen, Leo 72
Jaguaribe, Helio 72
Jantsch, Erich 33
Jefferson, Ray 55
Jessop, W.N. 32, 84
Johnston, John 97
Jones, Holway R. 127
Junghans, Karl H. 73

K

Kahn, Alfred J. 36
Kain, John F. 109
Kalba, Kas 32
Kalton, G. 92
Kaplan, Abraham B. 81
Kaplan, Marshall 43, 44, 63
Kaser, Michael 73
Kendig, Hal 94
Kent, T.J. 122
Kettle, Peter 37, 111
Kilbridge, Maurice 102
Kish, Leslie 92
Klaasen, Leo H. 33
Klein, Burton H. 22
Koontz, Harold 59
Kozlowski, J. 111
Kramer, Ralph M. 63
Krieger, Martin H. 33
Krueckeberg, Donald A. 48, 81
Krumholz, Norman 55
Krutilla, John 114
Kulski, Julian 11

L

Lamone, Rudolph P. 97

Author Index

Author Index

TITLE INDEX

This index is alphabetized letter by letter and references are to page numbers. In some cases the titles have been shortened.

Title Index

Title Index

Title Index

Title Index

SUBJECT INDEX

This index is alphabetized letter by letter and references are to page numbers. Underlined page numbers refer to main areas within the subject.

Subject Index

modernization of 7
planning and development in 35
Brace, C. C. 4
Brandywine watershed area (Pa.) 57
Brazil, planning and development in
    71, 72-73
Budgeting and finance in planning
    54, 123-24, 125, 126
    relationship to policy analysis 55
Buildings, in regional planning 9
Bulgaria, comparative study of regional
    development in 67
Bureaucracy in planning 34, 44, 54,
    56
    changes needed in 46
    conflict with decentralized advo-
        cacy 65
    in developing countries 75
    failures of 42
    relationship to the political and
        corporate environments 68-69
Business planning. See Corporate
    planning

C

Calcutta, comparative studies of
    planning in 68
    planning and development in 72
California, application of science to
    policy issues in 47. See also
    Berkeley, Calif.; Contra Costa,
    County, Calif.; Los Angeles;
    Oakland, Calif.; San Diego;
    San Francisco; Santa Clara,
    Calif.; West Oakland, Calif.
Canada
    comparative studies of planning in
        66
    regional planning in 70
    See also Nova Scotia; Toronto
Capital, flow of 109
Capital expenditures. See Budgeting
    and finance
Capitalism, economic planning and
    73
Capital punishment, reality vs. judg-
    ments in 25
Carnegie school of organizational
    behavior 20

CDC. See Community development
    corporations
Census 93
    collection and its procedures 86
    statistical analyses of 94
    users guides to 87
Central America, planning and de-
    velopment in 75
Chicago
    community action programs in 65
    historic preservation in 121
    land use and transportation planning
        in 110
    planning and development in 53,
        66
    poverty programs in 63
    urban renewal in 112
Chicago Public Housing Authority 37
Chile, planning and development in
    72
China, planning and development in
    71
Cincinnati, history of urban planning
    in 3
Cities
    cultural role of 50
    history of 2-3, 4, 5, 6, 7
    physical structure and form of 3,
        4, 52
    politics of 34, 37
    See also Downtown and central
        city areas; Garden cities;
        Local government in urban
        planning; Megalopoly; Metro-
        politination; New towns;
        Planned towns
Citizen participation, in the planning
    process 35, 49, 61-66, 73
    See also Public choice theory
City managers, planning proposals
    and 55
City planning. See Urban planning
Cleveland
    effectiveness of manpower legisla-
        tion in 44
    planning and development in 55,
        56
Clients. See Citizen participation
Cluster analysis. See Statistics
Colombia, planning and development
    in 71

Colorado, land use planning in 47
Columbia, Md. 43
  participative planning in 62
Commerce
  interregional 126
  medieval 3
Committee of Regional Accounts of
    Resources for the Future 125
  conference (1960) 108
  second conference (1962) 107-8,
    126
Common Market. See European Eco-
    nomic Community
Community Action Programs 64
  evaluation of 117
Community development. See Neigh-
    borhood and community de-
    velopment
Community development corporations
    (CDC) 62
Commuters and commuting 109
Comprehensive Employment and Train-
    ing Act (1973) 44
Computer methods. See Simulation,
    modeling, and gaming theory;
    Systems theory and analysis
Conference on Urban Development
    Models (1967) 102
Conflict
  between decentralized and central-
    ized bureaucracies 65
  between professionals and clients
    64
  between programs and planning
    boards 55-56
  intra-neighborhood 65
  resolution of 33
Contra Costa County, Calif., poverty
    programs in 63
Corporate planning 58-61
  bibliography 59-60, 127
  multinational 60
Corrections. See Criminal justice
Cost-benefit analysis. See Economics
    of urban planning, evaluation
    tools in
Council of Planning Libraries 127
Coventry, England, planning and de-
    velopment in 84

CPM. See Critical Path Method
    (CPM)
Criminal justice system
  cost-benefit analysis in 113
  guides to community 88
  program evaluation in 117
  social indicators in 86
Critical Path Method (CPM), bibliog-
    raphy 128

D

Dade County, Fla., government of
    58
Data sources. See Information and
    information processing
Deaths, models of 96
Decision making and theory in plan-
    ning 82-83, 84
  analysis of governmental 46
  conflicts between professionals and
    clients 64
  forecasting and 105, 106
  individual and organizational 20-25,
    26, 28, 29, 41, 59, 61
  influence of environment in strategy
    of 30
  linear programming and 97-98
  models of 20, 21, 22, 24, 35
  in regional planning 49
  role of evaluation 37
  systems analysis and 96
Delaware Estuary model 39
Delaware River Basin Commission 49
Demography
  methodology of 96
  multi-regional mathematical 95-96
  in planning and development 52,
    69
  population growth aspects of 95
  See also Migration; Population;
    Urban geography
Department of Health, Education, and
    Welfare. See U.S. Depart-
    ment of Health, Education,
    and Welfare (HEW)
Department of Housing and Urban De-
    velopment. See U.S. Depart-
    ment of Housing and Urban
    Development (HUD)

Subject Index

costs in 119, 130
federal policies in 41, 43, 46–47
laws and regulations in 122
markets and location in 110
program evaluation in 117, 119
quality scales in 94
in regional planning 49
study guides to 88
systems analysis techniques in 84
See also Buildings
HUD. See U.S. Department of
Housing and Urban Development (HUD)
Humanism, in the planning process
81

I

Illinois. See Chicago
India, planning and development in
73. See also Calcutta
Industrialization, medieval 3
Industrial location 60, 109
in developing countries 74
Industry
development of 109
loans to, in regional development
51
Information and information processing
bibliography 128, 131
sources and indicators in 80, 85–
89
systems 55, 89-91
See also Social science research;
Statistics
Input-output analysis. See Systems
theory and analysis
Insurance, mortgage 46
Insurance companies, planning in 60
Interest groups
power of 54
social change and 56
in urban planning 34, 57
See also Property interests
Interests and goals 41
accounting for different in planning 31
of citizen participation groups 64
erosion of minority 42
social 86

See also Public choice theory;
Values
Interviewing techniques 92
Investment
application of operations research
to 97
cost–benefit analysis in public 113
Israel
planning and development in 68,
74
regional planning in 50
See also Jerusalem
Italy
planning and development in 73
urban planning in ancient 2

J

Japan, national economic planning
in 107
Jerusalem, planning and development
in 70
Job location 109. See also Employment
Job training, program evaluation in
117
Johnson, Lyndon Baines
housing policies under 46–47
Model Cities Programs under 6
new town development under 42
poverty programs under 7, 43
program budgeting under 115

K

Kallang Basin Reclamation Project
(Singapore) 72
Karachi, Pakistan, planning and de-
velopment in 72
Kentucky. See Lexington, Ky.;
Louisville, Ky.

L

Labor unions. See Trade unions
Lagos, Nigeria, comparative studies
of planning in 68
Land use planning and law 8, 13,
53, 54, 57, 110, 119-23
automated data systems in 55, 91

Subject Index

Subject Index